England's Best Loved Poems

England's Best Loved Poems

THE ENCHANTMENT OF ENGLAND

GEORGE COURTAULD

EBURY
PRESS
LONDON

13 5 7 9 10 8 6 4 2

Published in 2007 by Ebury Press, an imprint of Ebury Publishing

A Random House Group Company

Copyright © George Courtauld 2007

George Courtauld has asserted his right to be identified as the author of this
Work in accordance with the Copyright, Designs and Patents Act 1988

The Random House Group Limited Reg. No. 954009

Addresses for companies within the Random House Group can be found at:
www.randomhouse.co.uk

A CIP catalogue record for this book is available from the British Library

The Random House Group Limited makes every effort to ensure that the
papers used in its books are made from trees that have been legally sourced
from well-managed and credibly certified forests. Our paper procurement
policy can be found at: www.randomhouse.co.uk

To buy books by your favourite authors and register for offers visit
www.rbooks.co.uk

Typeset in Perpetua by Palimpsest Book Production Ltd,
Grangemouth, Stirlingshire

Printed and bound in Great Britain by CPI Mackays, Chatham ME5 8TD

ISBN 9780091909666

❧ CONTENTS ❧

[v]

3: LOVE

4: WONDER

5: THE UNDERDOG

6: PRAYER

7: MAGIC

8: DEFIANCE

9: KINGSHIP

10: LOSS

11: HOME

INTRODUCTION

ENGLAND IS ENCHANTED – its landscape, history and traditions, and especially its people; their gallantry, generosity, modesty and eccentricity – an enchantment given unique expression through our poetry.

Why is it that poetry can move us so — even 'bad' poetry, even doggerel? Coleridge described poetry as 'the best words in the best order' but it can be so much more than this. It can be a kind of déjà vu, a catch in the throat, articulating heart-breakingly familiar feelings in a way that enables lines not heard or remembered for decades, or heard for the first time, to make our hair stand on end or bring tears to our eyes.

Perhaps it is because, though many things trigger our sense of belonging, one of the most potent and earliest is poetry: the shared chanting of verse. The image of a mother singing or reciting to her child is universal and the repetition of those childhood songs and nursery rhymes not only teaches us to interact with those around us, but provides some of our earliest experiences of joining in, as well as strengthening our grasp of language.

The language of England is part of its enchantment, the common heritage of us all, fashioned, tested and refined by the generations as they hacked out our glorious national story. And it is through their literature and poetry that those great English men and women of our past still bare their souls, that their attitudes and aspirations still echo down the ages, their hopes, their heartbreak, their very humanity, set down in shining verse.

I was lucky enough to have a childhood steeped in poetry, or at any rate verse. My mother would 'declaim' anything from Shakespeare to A. A. Milne, and my father used to write to us at boarding school in rhyme. Neither my brother nor I were very good at games and I remember being immensely cheered, after a particularly harsh run-in with the games master, to receive a sympathetic letter from my father with a chorus beginning, 'Hoppity, Skippity, Crutch'.

As a rather dozy, inarticulate child, it was not until school that I was first mesmerised by the Book of Common Prayer, the King James Bible and Hymns Ancient and Modern. This seemed to me to be the language of Titans, though it somehow never occurred to me then to sit down and study it. It was only when I had children of my own that I consciously set out to learn poetry by heart.

On the birth of our first child, in a spasm of fatherly zeal, I asked my wife if I might take over the late night feeds. She left a bottle of milk in the fridge and when the baby woke, normally around two in the morning, I'd warm up the milk in the microwave, give him the bottle, wind him and put him back to bed. This was a procedure that somehow left me fizzing with energy, despite the late hour, and afterwards I often found myself lying awake, increasingly desperate to drift off before the alarm went and increasingly less able to do so.

My wife kindly offered to take over the nightly feeds again but, apart from actually wanting to do my bit, I was also reluctant to fail almost the first test of my fatherhood. I found the solution in poetry. I printed off enlarged photocopies of poems I half remembered and had once thought amazing, and while my son noisily enjoyed his requisite X ounces every night, I would read him a poem over and over again. Having returned to bed, I would then recite it back to myself in my head, not allowing myself to even think about sleep until I had it word perfect: I was often out like a light before finishing the first verse.

It is those poems learnt during the infancy of my three sons, and continued on my morning train journeys to London, that form the core of this book. So this is a very personal selection, the criteria for inclusion being primarily that the lines are important to me. And to me, like the vast majority of us, my sense of community, of Englishness, is of profound importance. Accordingly, I have included hymns, marches, songs and psalms that are commonly recited or sung together, kindling and sustaining our sense of belonging.

There are also pieces that relate to our communal past, affirming our joint involvement in events like The Charge of the Light Brigade, Agincourt, and The Execution of Charles I. And there are those that are quite simply so much admired and so well known that they must be numbered among the jewels in the crown of our common heritage.

But, of course, there are also some very intimate and private poems here in which authors explore specific personal feelings, triumphs and tragedies: Kipling on the loss of his son, for example, and Milton on his blindness, or Raleigh on the eve of his execution. These poems contain some of the greatest lines ever written.

Poetry is created by individuals and an indication of the life and times of the writer can enormously enhance our appreciation of their work, so I have added brief biographical notes on each. I have also added the date of publication of each poem or, where possible, the date it was written. They have been grouped into chapters as they do seem to follow clearly discernible themes – themes with a very English resonance.

It has been immense fun putting this book together. I do hope it is as much fun to read. In the words of one of the authors featured in this anthology, W. H. Auden, poetry may 'make nothing happen' but it certainly encapsulates everything that matters.

FELLOWSHIP

THE ENGLISH GIFT for fellowship is based on the love of people in all their quirkiness, diversity and eccentricity. I believe it is this affection, this English faith in our fellows, that has fostered the creation of so many clubs, societies, companies and movements – 'fellow-ships', which over the generations have been such a terrific force for progress and continuity, justice and self-expression.

All the poems in this chapter reflect that great English sense of mellow inclusion, whether it be sitting together on a train or belting out 'The Old Hundredth'.

Adlestrop
1917
EDWARD THOMAS

EDWARD THOMAS WAS born in London in 1878 and went to Oxford where, very unusually in those days, he got married while he was still a student. He earned an unpredictable living as a freelance journalist. He met the American poet Robert Frost just before the outbreak of the First World War. Frost inspired him to start writing poetry himself, though very little was published before he was killed in action in 1917, aged 39.

I used to take the train from Essex to the West Country to go to school and since 1990 I have commuted up to London by train. The patience, tolerance, kindness and camaraderie of my fellow travellers over the years seems to exemplify what one philosopher described as the unconscious English 'fellowship of strangers'.

Yes, I remember Adlestrop —
The name, because one afternoon
Of heat the express-train drew up there
Unwontedly. It was late June.

The steam hissed. Someone cleared his throat.
No one left and no one came
On the bare platform. What I saw
Was Adlestrop — only the name —

And willows, willow-herb, and grass,
And meadowsweet, and haycocks dry;
No whit less still and lonely fair
Than the high cloudlets in the sky.

And for that minute a blackbird sang
Close by, and round him, mistier,
Farther and farther, all the birds
Of Oxfordshire and Gloucestershire.

Heart of Oak
—→ 1760 ⇐—

Words: DAVID GARRICK
Music: DR WILLIAM BOYCE

THE OAK HAS a special place in our history. It was revered by the ancient Druids; Robin Hood and Charles II both found refuge in its branches; and it was under an oak tree that Elizabeth I first learned of her accession to the throne. It was also the wood from which our great fleets were constructed from the time of Alfred the Great until the middle of the nineteenth century.

'Heart of Oak' is the official march of both the Royal Navy and the Royal Canadian Navy. The 'wonderful year' mentioned in the first verse refers to the 12-month period from 1759 to 1760 during the Seven Years War, when British forces were victorious over the French at Quebec, Quiberon Bay and Minden.

The Master of the King's Band of Musicians and Organist of the Chapel Royal, Dr William Boyce, composed the music. The words were written by David Garrick. Garrick was a pupil of Dr Johnson and left Lichfield for London with him in 1737. He became a celebrated actor-manager and he ran the Drury Lane Theatre from 1747 to 1776. He died in 1779 and is the last actor to have been buried in Westminster Abbey.

Come, cheer up, my lads, 'tis to glory we steer,
To add something more to this wonderful year;
To honour we call you, as freemen not slaves,
For who are as free as the sons of the waves?

Chorus:
Heart of oak are our ships, jolly tars are our men,
We always are ready; steady, boys, steady!
We'll fight and we'll conquer again and again.

We ne'er see our foes but we wish them to stay,
They never see us but they wish us away;
If they run, why we follow, and run them ashore,
And if they won't fight us, we cannot do more.

Chorus . . .

They swear they'll invade us, these terrible foes,
They frighten our women, our children and beaus,
But should their flat bottoms in darkness get o'er,
Still Britons they'll find to receive them on shore.

Chorus . . .

Britannia triumphant, her ships sweep the sea,
Her standard is Justice — her watchword, 'be free.'
Then cheer up, my lads, with one heart let us sing,
Our soldiers, our sailors, our statesmen, and King.

Chorus . . .

I Vow to Thee, My Country
⟹ 1918 ⟸

Words: SIR CECIL SPRING-RICE
Music: GUSTAV HOLST

SIR CECIL SPRING-RICE was a diplomat who, after Eton and Oxford, entered the Foreign Office. He spent time in Berlin, Cairo, Persia and Sweden and from 1913 to 1918 he was the British ambassador in Washington DC. His charm and tact were credited with helping to persuade the US to join the Allies in the First World War.

Gustav Holst, Professor of Composition at the Royal College of Music, was born in Cheltenham and educated at the Grammar School there, where he excelled at the trombone. Holst and Spring-Rice's daughters both attended St Paul's Girls School and, in 1925, Holst married Spring-Rice's words to 'Jupiter' from his *Planets Suite*. In August 2004, the Right Reverend Stephen Lowe, Bishop of Hulme, condemned the hymn as 'totally heretical' and called for it to be banned from Anglican ceremonies on the grounds that it set national above religious loyalties. He was largely ignored. The hymn was sung at the funeral of Diana, Princess of Wales, having been sung at her wedding at her personal request.

It remains a hymn still loved by millions, the sentiments it expresses explained by the date of its composition: the end of the First World War when the whole country was desperately seeking justification for the sacrifice of an entire generation.

I vow to thee, my country, all earthly things above,
Entire and whole and perfect, the service of my love:
The love that asks no question, the love that stands the test,
That lays upon the altar the dearest and the best;
The love that never falters, the love that pays the price,
The love that makes undaunted the final sacrifice.

And there's another country, I've heard of long ago,
Most dear to them that love her, most great to them that know;
We may not count her armies, we may not see her King;
Her fortress is a faithful heart, her pride is suffering;
And soul by soul and silently her shining bounds increase,
And her ways are ways of gentleness and all her paths are peace.

Song of the Western Men
⇒ 1825 ⇐

Words: R. S. HAWKER
Music: CORNISH TRADITIONAL

THIS SONG IS popularly regarded as the Cornish national anthem. It was published anonymously in 1825, although the core three lines – 'And shall Trelawny die?/Here's twenty thousand Cornish men/Will know the reason why!' – were first recorded in 1688. This was when the Catholic King, James II, indicted seven bishops, including John Trelawny, who was then the Bishop of Bristol, for seditious libel. The men were imprisoned in the Tower of London and I had always assumed that Trelawny was executed there but he was in fact acquitted of all charges. He went on to become Bishop of Exeter and then Winchester.

R. S. Hawker wrote the lyrics to the 'Song of the Western Men' when he was an undergraduate at Oxford, by which time he was already an accomplished poet. In 1834 he became vicar of Morwenstow in north Cornwall, where he developed his interest in Cornish life and culture. His epic poem based on the Arthurian legend, The Quest of the Sangraal, contains passages of 'visionary power' that have been attributed to his opium addiction. He converted to Roman Catholicism on his deathbed in 1875.

> A good sword and a trusty hand!
> A merry heart and true!
> King James's men shall understand
> What Cornish lads can do!
>
> And have they fixed the where and when?
> And shall Trelawny die?
> Here's twenty thousand Cornish men
> Will know the reason why!

Out spake their captain brave and bold,
    A merry wight was he:
'If London Tower were Michael's hold,
    We'd set Trelawny free!

'We'll cross the Tamar, land to land,
    The Severn is no stay,
With 'one and all,' and hand in hand;
    And who shall bid us nay?

'And when we come to London Wall,
    A pleasant sight to view,
Come forth! come forth! ye cowards all,
    Here's men as good as you.

'Trelawny he's in keep and hold,
    Trelawny he may die;
But here's twenty thousand Cornish bold
    Will know the reason why!'

Everyone Sang

1919

SIEGFRIED SASSOON

AFTER MARLBOROUGH and Cambridge and winning a Military Cross during his first spell on the front line, Siegfried Sassoon's contempt for his military superiors was a shock to the British public. He was reputed to have thrown away his MC and was packed off to hospital with shell-shock, where he met Wilfred Owen and organised a public protest against the continuation of the war. A great sportsman, he loved hunting and cricket. In 1957, aged 69, he became a Roman Catholic. He died ten years later.

Everyone suddenly burst out singing;
And I was filled with such delight
As prisoned birds must find in freedom
Winging wildly across the white
Orchards and dark-green fields; on — on — and out of sight.

Everyone's voice was suddenly lifted,
And beauty came like the setting sun:
My heart was shaken with tears; and horror
Drifted away . . . O, but Everyone
Was a bird; and the song was wordless; the singing will
    never be done.

Land of Hope and Glory
―――→ 1902 ――――

Words: A. C. BENSON
Music: EDWARD ELGAR

THE HYMN-WRITER A. C. Benson was the son of an archbishop of Canterbury. He wrote the words to 'Land of Hope and Glory' when he was a housemaster at Eton. The rousing music is Edward Elgar's first Pomp and Circumstance March, which formed part of his 'Coronation Ode' in honour of Edward VII.

Of course we are a land of hope and glory. Many now think of this as the unofficial English, rather than British, national anthem.

> Dear Land of Hope, thy hope is crowned.
> God make thee mightier yet!
> On Sov'ran brows, beloved, renowned,
> Once more thy crown is set.
> Thine equal laws, by Freedom gained,
> Have ruled thee well and long;
> By Freedom gained, by Truth maintained,
> Thine Empire shall be strong.
>
> Land of Hope and Glory,
> Mother of the Free,
> How shall we extol thee,
> Who are born of thee?
> Wider still and wider
> Shall thy bounds be set;
> God, who made thee mighty,
> Make thee mightier yet.
> (God, who made thee mighty,
> Make thee mightier yet.)

Thy fame is ancient as the days,
As Ocean large and wide:
A pride that dares, and heeds not praise,
A stern and silent pride:
Not that false joy that dreams content
With what our sires have won;
The blood a hero sire hath spent
Still nerves a hero son.

Land of Hope and Glory, etc.

Psalm 100

1561

Scottish Metrical Version

THIS IS ONE of those pieces where it is impossible to disso-
ciate the words from the tune that traditionally accompanies
it, attributed to Louis Bourgeois. Being part of a congregation
singing this at the top of one's lungs (and anticipating the deep
rumble of the organ at the end of each verse) is a soul-stirring
experience. Like the other great psalm that the British have taken
to their hearts, the 23rd, this one uses the imagery of sheep and
shepherds.

All people that on earth do dwell,
Sing to the Lord with cheerful voice.
Him serve with mirth, His praise forth tell;
Come ye before Him and rejoice.

Know that the Lord is God indeed;
Without our aid He did us make:
We are His flock, He doth us feed,
And for His sheep He doth us take.

O enter then His gates with praise;
Approach with joy His courts unto:
Praise, laud, and bless His name always,
For it is seemly so to do.

For why? the Lord our God is good.
His mercy is for ever sure;
His truth at all times firmly stood,
And shall from age to age endure.

Rule, Britannia
1740

Words: JAMES THOMSON
Music: DR THOMAS ARNE

JAMES THOMSON, the son of a minister, was educated at Edinburgh. He moved to London in 1725, aged 25, and became a hugely influential, patriotic poet. Rule, Britannia first appeared in *Alfred*, a masque he wrote, in 1740.

Famed for his 'unashamed idleness', Coleridge nevertheless described Thomson as a 'great poet rather than a good one', and Wordsworth believed he was the greatest poetical innovator since Milton. His poems also inspired many of Turner's pictures.

The Romans referred to what is now England, Wales and Scotland as Britannia, the inhabitants having been known as the Pritani or Priteni since the fourth century BC. The term was first used officially in English in 1604, when James I was proclaimed the King of Great Britain. The image of Britannia as a woman resting on a shield first appeared on a coin of Antoninus Pius in around AD 160. She reappeared on a Charles II copper penny in 1665, when the model was Frances Stewart, later the Duchess of Richmond.

The music was written by the Old Etonian composer to Drury Lane Theatre, Dr Thomas Arne.

> When Britain first, at Heaven's command,
> Arose from out the azure main,
> This was the charter of the land,
> And guardian angels sung this strain:
>   'Rule, Britannia! Britannia rule the waves;
>   Britons never, never, never shall be slaves.'

The nations, not so blest as thee,
Must, in their turns, to tyrants fall;
While thou shalt flourish great and free,
The dread and envy of them all.
    'Rule, Britannia!' etc.

Still more majestic shalt thou rise,
More dreadful, from each foreign stroke;
As the loud blast that tears the skies
Serves but to root thy native oak.
    'Rule, Britannia!' etc.

Thee haughty tyrants ne'er shall tame;
All their attempts to bend thee down
Will but arouse thy generous flame,
And work their woe and thy renown.
    'Rule, Britannia!' etc.

To thee belongs the rural reign;
Thy cities shall with commerce shine;
All thine shall be the subject main,
And every shore it circles thine.
    'Rule, Britannia!' etc.

The Muses, still with Freedom found,
Shall to thy happy coast repair:
Blest isle, with matchless beauty crowned,
And manly hearts to guard the fair.
    'Rule, Britannia!' etc.

The Charge of the Light Brigade
1854

ALFRED, LORD TENNYSON

ALFRED, LORD TENNYSON was born in Lincolnshire in 1809 and educated at Cambridge. In 1850, on the death of Wordsworth, he was appointed Poet Laureate. He married soon after and spent the rest of his life on the Isle of Wight and in Surrey.

The Crimean War (1854–56) was fairly inconclusive and, with the first war reporter, William Russell, writing for *The Times* and Florence Nightingale exposing the horrific conditions in military hospitals, it provided very little to cheer the British public. The Charge of the Light Brigade was a blunder and achieved very little but even their enemies admired the staggering resolve and gallantry of the British cavalrymen.

Our great British institutions – regiments, schools, hospitals and universities – and the fellowship that they embody, despite everything the government can throw at them, remain the envy of the world.

> Half a league, half a league,
>   Half a league onward,
> All in the valley of Death
>   Rode the six hundred.
> 'Forward, the Light Brigade!
> Charge for the guns!' he said:
> Into the valley of Death
>   Rode the six hundred.

'Forward, the Light Brigade!'
Was there a man dismay'd?
Not tho' the soldier knew
   Some one had blunder'd:
Their's not to make reply,
Their's not to reason why,
Their's but to do and die:
Into the valley of Death
   Rode the six hundred.

Cannon to right of them,
Cannon to left of them,
Cannon in front of them
   Volley'd and thunder'd;
Storm'd at with shot and shell,
Boldly they rode and well,
Into the jaws of Death,
Into the mouth of Hell
   Rode the six hundred.

Flash'd all their sabres bare,
Flash'd as they turn'd in air
Sabring the gunners there,
Charging an army, while
   All the world wonder'd:
Plunged in the battery-smoke
Right thro' the line they broke;
Cossack and Russian
Reel'd from the sabre-stroke
   Shatter'd and sunder'd.
Then they rode back, but not
   Not the six hundred.

Cannon to right of them,
Cannon to left of them,
Cannon behind them
   Volley'd and thunder'd;
Storm'd at with shot and shell,
While horse and hero fell,
They that had fought so well
Came thro' the jaws of Death,
Back from the mouth of Hell,
All that was left of them,
   Left of six hundred.

When can their glory fade?
O the wild charge they made!
   All the world wonder'd.
Honour the charge they made!
Honour the Light Brigade,
   Noble six hundred!

REGRET

DISAPPOINTMENT, RESIGNATION, NOSTALGIA and regret are all great poetic spurs. In this chapter I have included examples ranging from the jokey to the desperate to the downright bitter. All of these poems contain an element of resignation, an acceptance of the situation, however dire, and none suggests any kind of solution.

Our national propensity to endure, to soldier on, to make the best of things, can perhaps be regarded as a weakness as well as a strength but it has stood us in great stead during times of national emergency.

Elegy
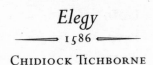
1586

CHIDIOCK TICHBORNE

CHIDIOCK TICHBORNE was arrested for his involvement in the Babington plot to assassinate Queen Elizabeth I and replace her with Mary Queen of Scots. He pleaded guilty and was executed in 1586. Almost nothing else is known about him and none of his other verse survives. This poem was found in his cell after his death.

My prime of youth is but a frost of cares,
    My feast of joy is but a dish of pain,
My crop of corn is but a field of tares,
    And all my good is but vain hope of gain;
        My life is fled, and yet I saw no sun,
        And now I live, and now my life is done.

The spring is past, and yet it hath not sprung;
    The fruit is dead, and yet the leaves be green,
My youth is gone and yet I am but young;
    I saw the world and yet I was not seen;
        My thread is cut and yet it is not spun;
        And now I live, and now my life is done.

I sought my death and found it in my womb,
    I looked for life and saw it was a shade,
I trod the earth and knew it was my tomb,
    And now I die, and now I am but made;
        My glass is full, and now my glass is run,
        And now I live, and now my life is done.

Going, Going

1974

PHILIP LARKIN

PHILIP LARKIN was born and brought up in Coventry, went to Oxford, and was the librarian of Hull University for 30 years. He gave up writing poetry almost completely in the late 1970s, saying 'the compulsion' had left him, asserting that he 'would rather write no poems than bad poems'. Accordingly, he declined the offer of Poet Laureateship in 1984.

'Going, Going' appeared in his third collection of verse, *High Windows*, ten years before he died. Larkin had the peculiarly English habit of writing off and decrying what he loved and the very human fear of the strange and new. And yet he did love and believe in love, ending his poem 'An Arundel Tomb' with the words, 'what will survive us is love'.

> I thought it would last my time —
> The sense that, beyond the town,
> There would always be fields and farms,
> Where the village louts could climb
> Such trees as were not cut down;
> I knew there'd be false alarms
>
> In the papers about old streets
> And split level shopping, but some
> Have always been left so far;
> And when the old part retreats
> As the bleak high-risers come
> We can always escape in the car.

Things are tougher than we are, just
As earth will always respond
However we mess it about;
Chuck filth in the sea, if you must:
The tides will be clean beyond.
   — But what do I feel now? Doubt?

Or age, simply? The crowd
Is young in the M1 cafe;
Their kids are screaming for more —
More houses, more parking allowed,
More caravan sites, more pay.
On the Business Page, a score

Of spectacled grins approve
Some takeover bid that entails
Five per cent profit (and ten
Per cent more in the estuaries): move
Your works to the unspoilt dales
(Grey area grants)! And when

You try to get near the sea
In summer . . .
It seems, just now,
To be happening so very fast;
Despite all the land left free
For the first time I feel somehow
That it isn't going to last,

That before I snuff it, the whole
Boiling will be bricked in
Except for the tourist parts —
First slum of Europe: a role
It won't be hard to win,
With a cast of crooks and tarts.

And that will be England gone,
The shadows, the meadows, the lanes,
The guildhalls, the carved choirs.
There'll be books; it will linger on
In galleries; but all that remains
For us will be concrete and tyres.

Most things are never meant.
This won't be, most likely; but greeds
And garbage are too thick-strewn
To be swept up now, or invent
Excuses that make them all needs.
I just think it will happen, soon.

He Never Expected Much
⟹ 1928 ⟸

THOMAS HARDY

THOMAS HARDY WAS born in Dorset in 1840, educated there and articled to an architect in Dorchester at the age of 16. He moved to London but gave up architecture in the 1860s in order to write full-time. He published the first of his 19 novels, *Desperate Remedies*, in 1871 and his last, *Jude the Obscure*, in 1896. He began publishing his poetry in 1898 and continued to write until his death in 1928.

> Well, World, you have kept faith with me,
> Kept faith with me;
> Upon the whole you have proved to be
> Much as you said you were.
> Since as a child I used to lie
> Upon the leaze and watch the sky,
> Never, I own, expected I
> That life would all be fair.
>
> 'Twas then you said, and since have said,
> Times since have said,
> In that mysterious voice you shed
> From clouds and hills around:
> 'Many have loved me desperately,
> Many with smooth serenity,
> While some have shown contempt of me
> Till they dropped underground.

'I do not promise overmuch,
Child; overmuch;
Just neutral-tinted haps and such,'
You said to minds like mine.
Wise warning for your credit's sake!
Which I for one failed not to take,
And hence could stem such strain and ache
As each year might assign.

'I look into my glass'
⟹ 1928 ⟸

THOMAS HARDY

I look into my glass,
And view my wasting skin,
And say, 'Would God it came to pass
My heart had shrunk as thin!'

For then, I, undistrest
By hearts grown cold to me,
Could lonely wait my endless rest
With equanimity.

But Time, to make me grieve,
Part steals, lets part abide;
And shakes this fragile frame at eve
With throbbings of noontide.

'I wake and feel the fell of dark . . .'

⟹ 1885 ⟸

GERARD MANLEY HOPKINS

GERARD MANLEY HOPKINS was born in London in 1844 and converted to Catholicism at Oxford. He entered the Jesuit novitiate in 1868 and was ordained in 1877, serving as a priest until he went to Stonyhurst in 1882 to teach Latin and Greek. He eventually became professor of Greek at University College, Dublin, and remained there until his death in 1889. His poems were not published until the end of the First World War.

Learning this poem by heart gave me horrendous nightmares for three weeks.

I wake and feel the fell of dark, not day.
What hours, O what black hours we have spent
This night! what sights you, heart, saw; ways you went!
And more must, in yet longer light's delay.

With witness I speak this. But where I say
Hours I mean years, mean life. And my lament
Is cries countless, cries like dead letters sent
To dearest him that lives alas! away.

I am gall, I am heartburn. God's most deep decree
Bitter would have me taste: my taste was me;
Bones built in me, flesh filled, blood brimmed the curse.

Selfyeast of spirit a dull dough sours. I see
The lost are like this, and their scourge to be
As I am mine, their sweating selves; but worse.

Remembrance

⟹ 1557 ⟸

SIR THOMAS WYATT

I ALWAYS THOUGHT SIR Thomas Wyatt's positions as 'Esquire to the King's Body' (Henry VIII) and 'Clerk to the King's Jewels' sounded rather fun and he does seem to have had an exciting life. Born in Kent around 1503, he went to Cambridge, accompanied the English ambassador to the papal court, became High Marshal of Calais, a privy councillor and lover to Anne Boleyn before her marriage. He was imprisoned on charges of adultery with her in 1536, subsequently pardoned and then knighted. He was ambassador to Spain and France and went on diplomatic missions all over Europe. He was imprisoned in the Tower of London for 'papist tendencies' but then cleared. Perhaps his greatest claim to fame was that he introduced the sonnet to England from Italy. Having been appointed High Steward of the King's Manor, he died in 1542.

The predatory tone of the first verse, the wistfulness of the second and the gentle exasperation of the third are enchanting. This poem, like all of Wyatt's verse, was published posthumously.

They flee from me, that sometime did me seek
With naked foot, stalking in my chamber.
I have seen them gentle, tame, and meek,
That now are wild, and do not remember
That sometime they put themselves in danger
To take bread at my hand; and now they range
Busily seeking with a continual change.

Thanked be fortune it hath been otherwise
   Twenty times better; but once, in special,
In thin array, after a pleasant guise,
     When her loose gown from her shoulders did fall,
     And she me caught in her arms long and small,
       Therewith all sweetly did me kiss
       And softly said, 'Dear heart, how like you this?'

It was no dream; I lay broad waking:
   But all is turned, thorough my gentleness,
Into a strange fashion of forsaking;
     And I have leave to go of her goodness,
     And she also to use newfangleness.
       But since that I so kindly am served,
       I would fain know what she hath deserved.

In Time of War (Sonnet VIII)
1938

W. H. AUDEN

W. H. AUDEN WAS born in Norfolk and went to Gresham's and then Oxford. He worked as a schoolmaster, travelled in Europe and China and then married to provide his wife with a British passport and save her from Nazi Germany. The marriage was never consummated. He went to Spain for two months to support the republicans in the Spanish Civil War but when Britain declared war on Germany in 1939 he moved to America, becoming a US citizen in 1946.

Although widely regarded as the greatest poet of his generation, he was resented in Britain for many years for what was regarded as his flight at a time of national peril.

After the death of his mother in 1941 he turned increasingly to Christianity, revisiting some of his earlier work and re-editing it accordingly. He returned to England and his old Oxford college shortly before his death in 1973, aged 67.

> He turned his field into a meeting-place,
> And grew the tolerant ironic eye,
> And formed the mobile money-changer's face,
> And found the notion of equality.
>
> And strangers were as brothers to his clocks,
> And with his spires he made a human sky;
> Museums stored his learning like a box,
> And paper watched his money like a spy.
>
> It grew so fast his life was overgrown,
> And he forgot what once it had been made for,
> And gathered into crowds and was alone,

And lived expensively and did without,
And could not find the earth which he had paid for,
Nor feel the love that he knew all about.

On His Blindness (Sonnet XVI)
══ 1673 ══

John Milton

MILTON WAS BORN three years before the King James Bible appeared in 1611. He was educated at St Paul's and Cambridge and, as a staunch parliamentarian, was appointed Secretary of Foreign Tongues to Cromwell's Council of State in 1649, a position he retained until the restoration of Charles II to the throne in 1660.

He became aware of his increasing blindness in 1650, when he began *Paradise Lost*, and was totally blind two years later. He finished *Paradise Lost* in 1663 and sold the copyright for £10. He was married three times and widowed twice.

Milton dismissed rhyme as 'but the invention of a barbarous age, to set off wretched matter and lame metre' and talked of 'the troublesome and modern bondage of rhyming', a sentiment he seems to have forgotten when writing this sonnet.

When I consider how my light is spent,
   Ere half my days, in this dark world and wide,
   And that one talent which is death to hide
   Lodged with me useless, though my soul more bent
To serve therewith my Maker, and present
   My true account, lest he returning chide,
   'Doth God exact day-labour, light denied?'
   I fondly ask. But Patience, to prevent
That murmur, soon replies: 'God doth not need
   Either man's work or his own gifts; who best
   Bear his mild yoke, they serve him best. His state
Is kingly: thousands at his bidding speed,
   And post o'er land and ocean without rest;
   They also serve who only stand and wait.'

Breadfruit
1962

PHILIP LARKIN

A GREAT UNCLE OF mine once quoted this poem when the whole family were solemnly sitting down to watch the film *Mutiny on the Bounty* with Marlon Brando. I must have been about eight and I remember thinking it was utter gobbledegook and wondering what on earth had prompted his recital – I now realise it was the breadfruit, of course.

Boys dream of native girls who bring breadfruit,
    Whatever they are,
As bribes to teach them how to execute
Sixteen sexual positions on the sand;
This makes them join (the boys) the tennis club,
Jive at the Mecca, use deodorants, and
On Saturdays squire ex-schoolgirls to the pub
    By private car.

Such uncorrected visions end in church
    Or registrar:
A mortgaged semi- with a silver birch;
Nippers; the widowed mum; having to scheme
With money; illness; age. So absolute
Maturity falls, when old men sit and dream
Of naked native girls who bring breadfruit,
    Whatever they are.

From The Garden of Proserpine
⟹ 1886 ⟸

ALGERNON CHARLES SWINBURNE

ALGERNON CHARLES SWINBURNE was born in 1837 and educated at Eton and Oxford. His 'wonderful rhythmic invention' was praised by Tennyson, and even Queen Victoria thought he might be the finest poet in her realm. However, rumours of his drinking and masochism, his support for Italian independence, along with other Pre-Raphaelites, and his aggressive ridicule of Christianity precluded any chance of his acceptance by the establishment.

In 1879, at the age of 40 and on the verge of physical and emotional collapse, Swinburne moved into the house in Putney of his friend the novelist Theodore Watts-Dunton, who looked after him until he died in 1909.

> Here, where the world is quiet;
>   Here, where all trouble seems
> Dead winds' and spent waves' riot
>   In doubtful dreams of dreams;
> I watch the green field growing
> For reaping folk and sowing,
> For harvest-time and mowing,
>   A sleepy world of streams.
> I am tired of tears and laughter,
>   And men that laugh and weep;
> Of what may come hereafter
>   For men that sow to reap:
> I am weary of days and hours,
> Blown buds of barren flowers,
> Desires and dreams and powers
>   And everything but sleep.
> [. . .]

Pale, beyond porch and portal,
　　Crowned with calm leaves, she stands
Who gathers all things mortal
　　With cold immortal hands;
Her languid lips are sweeter
Than love's who fears to greet her
To men that mix and meet her
　　From many times and lands.
[. . .]
From too much love of living,
　　From hope and fear set free,
We thank with brief thanksgiving
　　Whatever gods may be
That no life lives for ever;
That dead men rise up never;
That even the weariest river
　　Winds somewhere safe to sea.
Then star nor sun shall waken,
　　Nor any change of light:
Nor sound of waters shaken,
　　Nor any sound or sight:
Nor wintry leaves nor vernal,
Nor days nor things diurnal;
Only the sleep eternal
　　In an eternal night.

3

LOVE

I READ SOMEWHERE THAT the earliest poetry addresses just three subjects – food, religion and romantic love – and indeed the association of poetry and poets with love must be almost as old as language itself.

Each of the poems in this chapter deals with romantic love in a different way: fantastical, matter-of-fact, light-hearted, breathless, inspirational and even terrifying. By accident rather than design, my selection concentrates exclusively on the joyous and the hopeful and fails to include a single poem about love lost.

To Mistress Margaret Hussey

1523

JOHN SKELTON

JOHN SKELTON WAS probably born in Yorkshire around 1460 and, having been educated at both Cambridge and Oxford, became official court poet in 1488. He was tutor to the future Henry VIII from 1494 to 1502, when he became Rector of Diss. His outspokenness and persistent ridicule of the rich and powerful, especially Cardinal Wolsey, led to his exile from London and even imprisonment, on occasion. He lived in Westminster from 1511 and became the King's Orator.

Much of Skelton's work is obscure, feisty and frantic but he could also be simple and tender. The comparison between a good and lovely woman and a bird of prey, the idea that a falcon should be considered gentle, does seem rather strange, but this is a sweet recital of Margaret Hussey's virtues and his regard for her.

I read this to my youngest son who said, 'That's not a poem, it's a list.'

> Merry Margaret,
> As midsummer flower,
> Gentle as falcon
> Or hawk of the tower:
> With solace and gladness,
> Much mirth and no madness,
> All good and no badness;
> So joyously,
> So maidenly,
> So womanly,
> Her demeaning
> In everything,
> Far, far passing

That I can indite,
 Or suffice to write
Of Merry Margaret,
 As midsummer flower,
Gentle as falcon
Or hawk of the tower.
 As patient and as still
And as full of good will
As fair Isaphill,
Coriander,
Sweet pomander,
Good Cassander,
Steadfast of thought,
Well made, well wrought,
Far may be sought
Ere that ye can find
So courteous, so kind,
As Merry Margaret,
 This midsummer flower,
Gentle as falcon
Or hawk of the tower.

Lovesong
⟶ 1976 ⟸
TED HUGHES

A YORKSHIREMAN EDUCATED AT Cambridge, Ted Hughes was a countryman whose love of nature was kindled by his passion for shooting and fishing as a boy. His energetic, innovative poetry is sometimes brutal, a reflection of what he saw as the innocent savagery of nature.

Hughes' life was filled with appalling tragedy. His first wife, the poet Sylvia Plath, committed suicide, as did his second wife, who also killed their daughter at the same time. He was Poet Laureate from 1984 until his death in 1998.

He loved her and she loved him
His kisses sucked out her whole past and future or tried to
He had no other appetite
She bit him she gnawed him she sucked
She wanted him complete inside her
Safe and sure forever and ever
Their little cries fluttered into the curtains

Her eyes wanted nothing to get away
Her looks nailed down his hands his wrists his elbows
He gripped her hard so that life
Should not drag her from that moment
He wanted all future to cease
He wanted to topple with his arms round her
Off that moment's brink and into nothing
Or everlasting or whatever there was

Her embrace was an immense press
To print him into her bones
His smiles were the garrets of a fairy palace
Where the real world would never come
Her smiles were spider bites
So he would lie still till she felt hungry
His words were occupying armies
Her laughs were an assassin's attempts
His looks were bullets daggers of revenge
His glances were ghosts in the corner with horrible secrets
His whispers were whips and jackboots
Her kisses were lawyers steadily writing
His caresses were the last hooks of a castaway
Her love-tricks were the grinding of locks
And their deep cries crawled over the floors
Like an animal dragging a great trap
His promises were the surgeon's gag
Her promises took the top off his skull
She would get a brooch made of it
His vows pulled out all her sinews
He showed her how to make a love-knot
Her vows put his eyes in formalin
At the back of her secret drawer
Their screams stuck in the wall

Their heads fell apart into sleep like the two halves
Of a lopped melon but love is hard to stop

In their entwined sleep they exchanged arms and legs
In their dreams their brains took each other hostage
In the morning they wore each other's face

Sonnet XLIII from Sonnets from the Portuguese
1850

ELIZABETH BARRETT BROWNING

ELIZABETH BARRETT BROWNING was born in 1806 and brought up in Herefordshire. In 1845 she began exchanging letters with the poet Robert Browning. They were married a year later in secret (her father had forbidden any of his 12 children to marry) and they fled to Italy, where they remained until her death in 1861.

Elizabeth's poetry was so highly regarded during her lifetime – far more so than her husband's – that she was proposed as the first female Poet Laureate when Wordsworth died in 1850. When it was realised that she would not return from Italy, the appointment was offered to Tennyson instead.

How do I love thee? Let me count the ways.
I love thee to the depth and breadth and height
My soul can reach, when feeling out of sight
For the ends of Being and ideal Grace.
I love thee to the level of everyday's
Most quiet need, by sun and candle-light.
I love thee freely, as men strive for Right;
I love thee purely, as they turn from Praise.
I love thee with the passion put to use
In my old griefs, and with my childhood's faith.
I love thee with a love I seemed to lose
With my lost saints, — I love thee with the breath,
Smiles, tears, of all my life! — and, if God choose,
I shall but love thee better after death.

'She walks in beauty . . .'

═══ 1815 ═══

GEORGE GORDON, LORD BYRON

'SHE MAY WALK in beauty, but I'll be damned if she'll take a walk with that poxy sot, George Byron,' an irate husband was reported to have said on hearing that these lines had been written about his wife. It is strange that Byron, the famous rake, who described a lie as 'but the truth in masquerade', should have been so attracted to innocence.

Born in London in 1788, he became the 6th Baron Byron in 1798 and was educated at Cambridge, where he published his first volumes of poetry. From 1809 to 1811 he travelled around the Mediterranean and published the first two cantos of *Childe Harold's Pilgrimage* in 1812 – to massive acclaim. 'I awoke one morning and found myself famous,' he said.

Byron married in 1815 but continued to have affairs with other women, possibly including his half-sister, Augusta. Leaving England as a result of the ensuing scandals, he went first to Switzerland and then to Italy. In 1823 he went to Greece to lend his support to the Greeks in their fight for independence He died there of fever in 1824, aged 36.

> She walks in beauty, like the night
> Of cloudless climes and starry skies;
> And all that's best of dark and bright
> Meet in her aspect and her eyes:
> Thus mellowed to that tender light
> Which heaven to gaudy day denies.
> One shade the more, one ray the less,
> Had half impaired the nameless grace
> Which waves in every raven tress,
> Or softly lightens o'er her face;

Where thoughts serenely sweet express
   How pure, how dear their dwelling-place.
And on that cheek, and o'er that brow,
   So soft, so calm, yet eloquent,
The smiles that win, the tints that glow,
   But tell of days in goodness spent,
A mind at peace with all below,
   A heart whose love is innocent.

The Visionary
1846

EMILY BRONTË

FROM THE AGE of two until her death at the age of 30, Emily
Brontë lived at Haworth in Yorkshire with her literary family.
Her sister Charlotte wrote *Jane Eyre* and she wrote *Wuthering Heights*.
It was Charlotte who persuaded Emily to publish her poems in
1845.

This poem seems to convey not only the isolated security of
her home but also a lurking threat – from whatever approaches
outside.

Silent is the house: all are laid asleep:
One alone looks out o'er the snow-wreaths deep,
Watching every cloud, dreading every breeze
That whirls the wildering drift, and bends the groaning trees.

Cheerful is the hearth, soft the matted floor;
Not one shivering gust creeps through pane or door;
The little lamp burns straight, its rays shoot strong and far:
I trim it well, to be the wanderer's guiding-star.

Frown, my haughty sire! chide, my angry dame;
Set your slaves to spy; threaten me with shame:
But neither sire nor dame, nor prying serf shall know,
What angel nightly tracks that waste of frozen snow.

What I love shall come like visitant of air,
Safe in secret power from lurking human snare;
Who loves me, no word of mine shall e'er betray,
Though for faith unstained my life must forfeit pay.

Burn, then, little lamp; glimmer straight and clear —
Hush! a rustling wing stirs, methinks, the air:
He for whom I wait, thus ever comes to me;
Strange Power! I trust thy might; trust thou my constancy.

A Subaltern's Love-song
⟹ 1945 ⟸
SIR JOHN BETJEMAN

BETJEMAN WAS EDUCATED at Marlborough and then Oxford, which he left without taking a degree, to become a school-master briefly, before taking up the post of Assistant Editor on the *Architectural Review*. His first poem, 'Death in Leamington', appeared in the *London Mercury* in 1930 and his first collection of verse, *Mount Zion*, was published in 1931.

Having worked as a film critic, editor, reviewer and broadcaster, he died a Knight, Poet Laureate and much-loved public person-ality, aged 78, in 1984.

Miss J. Hunter Dunn, Miss J. Hunter Dunn,
Furnish'd and burnish'd by Aldershot sun,
What strenuous singles we played after tea,
We in the tournament — you against me!

Love-thirty, love-forty, oh! weakness of joy,
The speed of a swallow, the grace of a boy,
With carefullest carelessness, gaily you won.
I am weak from your loveliness, Joan Hunter Dunn.

Miss Joan Hunter Dunn, Miss Joan Hunter Dunn,
How mad I am, sad I am, glad that you won.
The warm-handled racket is back in its press,
But my shock-headed victor, she loves me no less.

Her father's euonymus shines as we walk,
And swing past the summer-house, buried in talk,
And cool the verandah that welcomes us in
To the six-o'clock news and a lime-juice and gin.

The scent of the conifers, sound of the bath,
The view from my bedroom of moss-dappled path,
As I struggle with double-end evening tie,
For we dance at the Golf Club, my victor and I.

On the floor of her bedroom lie blazer and shorts
And the cream-coloured walls are be-trophied with sports,
And westering, questioning settles the sun
On your low-leaded window, Miss Joan Hunter Dunn.

The Hillman is waiting, the light's in the hall,
The pictures of Egypt are bright on the wall,
My sweet, I am standing beside the oak stair
And there on the landing's the light on your hair.

By roads 'not adopted', by woodlanded ways,
She drove to the club in the late summer haze,
Into nine-o'clock Camberley, heavy with bells
And mushroomy, pine-woody, evergreen smells.

Miss Joan Hunter Dunn, Miss Joan Hunter Dunn,
I can hear from the car-park the dance has begun.
Oh! full Surrey twilight! importunate band!
Oh! strongly adorable tennis-girl's hand!

Around us are Rovers and Austins afar,
Above us, the intimate roof of the car,
And here on my right is the girl of my choice,
With the tilt of her nose and the chime of her voice,

And the scent of her wrap, and the words never said,
And the ominous, ominous dancing ahead.
We sat in the car-park till twenty to one
And now I'm engaged to Miss Joan Hunter Dunn.

Meeting at Night
—— 1845 ——

ROBERT BROWNING

BARGING IN TO the wrong lecture at university one day, I listened enthralled as a visiting American professor explained how this poem reveals the author's sexist and sex-obsessive depravity. In fact, Browning appears to have been a thoroughly decent man who, living at home and being supported by his father, rescued his wife from her tyrannical father when he was 34, humbly accepted her pre-eminence while she was alive and then, after her death, himself became one of our greatest poets. The fact that he corresponded and became engaged to his wife in secret makes this poem all the more apt.

The gray sea and the long black land;
And the yellow half-moon large and low;
And the startled little waves that leap
In fiery ringlets from their sleep,
As I gain the cove with pushing prow,
And quench its speed i' the slushy sand.

Then a mile of warm sea-scented beach;
Three fields to cross till a farm appears;
A tap at the pane, the quick sharp scratch
And blue spurt of a lighted match,
And a voice less loud, through its joys and fears,
Than the two hearts beating each to each!

Sonnet XVIII

1595

WILLIAM SHAKESPEARE

BORN IN WARWICKSHIRE in 1564, Shakespeare was both a playwright and an actor and, out of necessity, was forced to direct his talent towards producing work that people would pay to see. However, his 152 sonnets were not written for profit and were probably produced during the 1590s.

> Shall I compare thee to a summer's day?
>> Thou art more lovely and more temperate:
> Rough winds do shake the darling buds of May,
>> And summer's lease hath all too short a date:
> Sometime too hot the eye of heaven shines,
>> And often is his gold complexion dimmed;
> And every fair from fair sometime declines,
>> By chance, or nature's changing course, untrimmed;
> But thy eternal summer shall not fade,
>> Nor lose possession of that fair thou owest;
> Nor shall Death brag thou wanderest in his shade,
>> When in eternal lines to time thou growest;
>>> So long as men can breathe, or eyes can see,
>>> So long lives this, and this gives life to thee.

The Sun Rising
—— 1603 ——

JOHN DONNE

JOHN DONNE, SOLDIER, lawyer, politician and eventually priest, was related to Sir Thomas More, the Lord Chancellor executed by Henry VIII in 1535 for his refusal to deny the authority of the Pope. (He was canonised in 1935.) Two of Donne's uncles, while wrangling over the ownership of one of More's teeth, were staggered when it miraculously split in two, allowing each to have half.

Donne was brought up a Catholic but became an Anglican in order to continue his education. After ruining his career by a secret marriage, he became a hugely successful Anglican vicar and Dean of St Paul's.

In this poem, he lives up to the label 'metaphysical', given to him by Dr Johnson for his use of 'far fetched comparisons', flippancy and 'scholastical quiddities', and berates the sun for disturbing him and his lover.

> Busy old fool, unruly Sun,
>   Why dost thou thus,
> Through windows, and through curtains call on us?
> Must to thy motions lovers' seasons run?
>   Saucy pedantic wretch, go chide
>   Late school-boys, and sour 'prentices,
>   Go tell court-huntsmen that the King will ride,
>   Call country ants to harvest offices;
> Love, all alike, no season knows, nor clime,
> Nor hours, days, months, which are the rags of time.

Thy beams, so reverend and strong
     Why shouldst thou think?
I could eclipse and cloud them with a wink,
But that I would not lose her sight so long:
    If her eyes have not blinded thine,
    Look, and to morrow late, tell me,
  Whether both the India's of spice and mine
  Be where thou left'st them, or lie here with me.
Ask for those Kings whom thou saw'st yesterday,
And thou shalt hear, 'All here in one bed lay.'

    She's all States, and all Princes I;
     Nothing else is.
Princes do but play us; compared to this,
All honour's mimic; all wealth alchemy.
    Thou, Sun, art half as happy as we,
    In that the world's contracted thus;
  Thine age asks ease, and since thy duties be
  To warm the world, that's done in warming us.
Shine here to us, and thou art everywhere;
This bed thy centre is, these walls, thy sphere.

4

WONDER

EXPERIENCING WONDER MUST be one of the great joys of being a living, thinking being. The ability to capture that experience in any medium, whether paint, words or music, and communicate it to others is surely a priceless talent.

All of these poems contain an element of religious awe and an awareness of the magnificence of nature: what Wordsworth would have called the 'sublime'.

Five of these poems explicitly mention God, and in all of them the poets seem conscious of a sense of being privileged and blessed to have had exposure or access to what they describe.

High Flight (An Airman's Ecstasy)

===> 1941 <===

JOHN GILLESPIE MAGEE

WHEN MY WIFE and I moved from London back to Essex in
1990, a great aunt invited us to tea. It was Remembrance
Sunday and she recounted how one summer's day, during the Battle
of Britain, she had had tea with three very young fighter pilots.
Within seven days all of them had been reported missing. She never
saw any of them again. Her husband was a tail-end Charlie in a
Lancaster bomber, (the rear gunner and reputedly the most
dangerous job in the RAF), but he survived the war. It was he
who introduced me to this poem.

John Gillespie Magee was an American airman who joined the
Royal Canadian Airforce when Britain declared war on Germany.
He was killed in action in 1941, aged 19.

Ronald Reagan recited this poem in his broadcast in 1986 after
the loss of the space shuttle Challenger with all its crew.

Oh! I have slipped the surly bonds of Earth
And danced the skies on laughter-silvered wings;
Sunward I've climbed, and joined the tumbling mirth
Of sun-split clouds, — and done a hundred things
You have not dreamed of — wheeled and soared and swung
High in the sunlit silence. Hov'ring there,
I've chased the shouting wind along, and flung
My eager craft through footless halls of air;
Up, up the long, delirious burning blue
I've topped the wind-swept heights with easy grace
Where never lark, or ever eagle flew —
And, while with silent, lifting mind I've trod
The high untrespassed sanctity of space,
Put out my hand, and touched the face of God.

Composed upon Westminster Bridge: September 3, 1802

──── 1802 ────

WILLIAM WORDSWORTH

IT WAS HIS love of nature that inspired Wordsworth to write poetry, which he described as 'the spontaneous overflow of powerful feelings . . . emotion recollected in tranquillity'. And he was susceptible to powerful feelings, describing it as bliss to be alive at the dawn of the French Revolution, and then wandering through France 'imbibing liberty'.

His revolutionary ardour eventually waned, however, and he settled in the Lake District in 1799, becoming the stamp distributor for Westmoreland in 1813, and Poet Laureate in 1843. He died in 1850, aged 80.

His attempts to create a less artificial and mannered poetry are credited with helping initiate the Romantic Movement. Here the wonder so often stimulated in him by mountains and wilderness is sparked by London, the creation of man.

> Earth has not anything to show more fair:
>   Dull would he be of soul who could pass by
>   A sight so touching in its majesty:
> This City now doth, like a garment, wear
> The beauty of the morning; silent, bare,
>   Ships, towers, domes, theatres, and temples lie
>   Open unto the fields, and to the sky;
> All bright and glittering in the smokeless air.
> Never did sun more beautifully steep
>   In his first splendour, valley, rock, or hill;
> Ne'er saw I, never felt, a calm so deep!
>   The river glideth at his own sweet will:
> Dear God! the very houses seem asleep;
>   And all that mighty heart is lying still!

The Tiger
1794
WILLIAM BLAKE

THE EMINENT QC John Beveridge credits William Blake with the finest four lines in English literature:

> To see a World in a Grain of Sand,
> And a Heaven in a Wild Flower,
> Hold Infinity in the palm of your hand,
> And Eternity in an hour.

(From *Auguries of Innocence,* 1803)

John Linnell, who supported Blake during the last decade of his life, described him as being 'sodden with wonder' and he does seem to have been a holy fool, despite his genius for poetry and illustration, and naive to the point of hopelessness. He was inspired by dreams and visions, clearly seeing many of the imaginary subjects he drew, like angels or the soul of a flea. When he died in 1827, aged 69, he was still delighting in and questioning everything.

> Tiger! Tiger! burning bright
> In the forests of the night,
> What immortal hand or eye
> Could frame thy fearful symmetry?
>
> In what distant deeps or skies
> Burned the fire of thine eyes?
> On what wings dare he aspire?
> What the hand dare seize the fire?

And what shoulder, and what art,
Could twist the sinews of thy heart?
And when thy heart began to beat,
What dread hand? And what dread feet?

What the hammer? What the chain?
In what furnace was thy brain?
What the anvil? What dread grasp
Dare its deadly terrors clasp?

When the stars threw down their spears,
And watered heaven with their tears,
Did he smile his work to see?
Did he who made the Lamb make thee?

Tiger! Tiger! burning bright
In the forests of the night,
What immortal hand or eye
Dare frame thy fearful symmetry?

To Autumn

=> 1820 <=

John Keats

BY THE TIME he was 15, in 1810, both of Keats's parents were dead. His guardian arranged for him to be apprenticed to a surgeon apothecary and he qualified in 1816 but he gave up medicine in order to write. He died of tuberculosis in Rome, aged 25.

Season of mists and mellow fruitfulness!
    Close bosom-friend of the maturing sun;
Conspiring with him how to load and bless
    With fruit the vines that round the thatch-eaves run;
To bend with apples the mossed cottage trees,
    And fill all fruit with ripeness to the core;
        To swell the gourd, and plump the hazel shells
With a sweet kernel; to set budding more,
    And still more, later flowers for the bees,
    Until they think warm days will never cease;
        For Summer has o'er-brimmed their clammy cells.

Who hath not seen thee oft amid thy store?
    Sometimes whoever seeks abroad may find
Thee sitting careless on a granary floor,
    Thy hair soft-lifted by the winnowing wind,
Or on a half-reaped furrow sound asleep,
    Drowsed with the fume of poppies, while thy hook
        Spares the next swath and all its twinèd flowers;
And sometimes like a gleaner thou dost keep
    Steady thy laden head across a brook;
    Or, by a cider-press, with patient look,
        Thou watchest the last oozings, hours by hours.

Where are the songs of Spring? Ay, where are they?
   Think not of them, thou hast thy music too, ——
While barred clouds bloom the soft-dying day,
   And touch the stubble-plains with rosy hue;
Then in a wailful choir the small gnats mourn
   Among the river-sallows, borne aloft
      Or sinking as the light wind lives or dies;
And full-grown lambs loud bleat from hilly bourn;
   Hedge-crickets sing; and now with treble soft
   The redbreast whistles from a garden-croft;
      And gathering swallows twitter in the skies.

The Windhover: To Christ Our Lord
1877

GERARD MANLEY HOPKINS

GERARD MANLEY HOPKINS believed that this was the best poem he ever wrote, a hymn of wonder at God's creation, inspired by the sight of a falcon.

I caught this morning morning's minion, King-
  dom of daylight's dauphin, dapple-dawn-drawn Falcon, in his
    riding
  Of the rolling level underneath him steady air, and striding
High there, how he rung upon the rein of a wimpling wing
In his ecstasy! then off, off forth on swing,
  As a skate's heel sweeps smooth on a bow-bend: the hurl and
    gliding
  Rebuffed the big wind. My heart in hiding
Stirred for a bird, — the achieve of, the mastery of the thing!

Brute beauty and valour and act, oh, air, pride, plume, here
  Buckle! AND the fire that breaks from thee then, a billion
Times told lovelier, more dangerous, O my chevalier!

  No wonder of it: sheer plod makes plough down sillion
Shine, and blue-bleak embers, ah my dear,
  Fall, gall themselves, and gash gold-vermilion.

God's Grandeur
1877

GERARD MANLEY HOPKINS

HERE HOPKINS ALSO uses the imagery of a bird that 'broods with warm breast and with ah! bright wings'.

The world is charged with the grandeur of God.
　It will flame out, like shining from shook foil;
　It gathers to a greatness, like the ooze of oil
Crushed. Why do men then now not reck his rod?
Generations have trod, have trod, have trod;
　And all is seared with trade; bleared, smeared with toil;
　And wears man's smudge and shares man's smell: the soil
Is bare now, nor can foot feel, being shod.

And for all this, nature is never spent;
　There lives the dearest freshness deep down things;
And though the last lights off the black West went
　Oh, morning, at the brown brink eastward, springs—
Because the Holy Ghost over the bent
　World broods with warm breast and with ah! bright wings.

From Hassan

=> 1922 <=

JAMES ELROY FLECKER

I WAS SHOCKED TO learn that James Elroy Flecker was only 31 when he died. *Hassan* and 'The Golden Journey to Samarkand' had always seemed to me so steeped in ancient wisdom and so perfectly crafted that I could not believe he wrote them and others at such an early age.

Having been to Uppingham and Oxford, Flecker entered the Consular Service in 1908 and was sent to Constantinople and Beirut, which confirmed his love of the East. He died of consumption in Switzerland in 1915 and *Hassan* was published seven years later.

In this extract from the verse play *Hassan*, the hero, Ishak, condemned to be executed at dawn, says these words to the Caliph as daybreak approaches. He is instantly pardoned.

Thy dawn, O Master of the world, thy dawn;
The hour the lilies open on the lawn,
The hour the grey wings pass beyond the mountains,
The hour of silence, when we hear the fountains,
The hour that dreams are brighter and winds colder,
The hour that young love wakes on a white shoulder,
O Master of the world, the Persian Dawn.

That hour, O Master, shall be bright for thee;
Thy merchants chase the morning down the sea,
The braves who fight thy war unsheathe the sabre,
The slaves who work thy mines are lashed to labour,
For thee the waggons of the world are drawn –
The ebony of night, the red of dawn!

The Sea and the Hills
⟹ 1903 ⟸
Rudyard Kipling

R UDYARD KIPLING WAS born in 1865 in Bombay and sent to
boarding school in Devon at the age of 5. On leaving the
United Services College, in 1882, he returned to India and worked
as a journalist in Lahore. Though he refused the Poet Laureateship
in 1895 and the Order of Merit three times, was a passionate Fran-
cophile and married to an American, he was regarded in his own
lifetime as the unofficial Poet Laureate of the Empire. He won the
Nobel Prize for Literature in 1907.

Who hath desired the Sea? – the sight of salt water unbounded
The heave and the halt and the hurl and the crash of the
    comber wind-hounded?
The sleek-barrelled swell before storm, grey, foamless, enor-
    mous, and growing —
Stark calm on the lap of the Line or the crazy-eyed hurricane
    blowing —
His Sea in no showing the same — his Sea and the same 'neath
    each showing:
His Sea as she slackens or thrills?
So and no otherwise — so and no otherwise hillmen desire
    their Hills!

Who hath desired the Sea? — the immense and contemptuous
    surges?
The shudder, the stumble, the swerve, as the star-stabbing
    bowsprit emerges?
The orderly clouds of the Trades, the ridged, roaring sapphire
thereunder —
Unheralded cliff-haunting flaws and the headsail's low-volleying
    thunder —

His Sea in no wonder the same — his Sea and the same through
  each wonder:
His Sea as she rages or stills?
So and no otherwise — so and no otherwise — hillmen desire
  their Hills.

Who hath desired the Sea? Her menaces swift as her mercies,
The in-rolling walls of the fog and the silver-winged breeze that
  disperses?
The unstable mined berg going South and the calvings and
  groans that declare it;
White water half-guessed overside and the moon breaking
  timely to bare it;
His Sea as his fathers have dared — his Sea as his children shall
  dare it:
His Sea as she serves him or kills?
So and no otherwise — so and no otherwise — hillmen desire
  their Hills.

Who hath desired the Sea? Her excellent loneliness rather
Than forecourts of Kings, and her outermost pits than the
  streets where men gather
Inland, among dust, under trees — inland where the slayer may
  slay him — Inland, out of reach of her arms, and the bosom
  whereon he must lay him —
His Sea from the first that betrayed — at the last that shall
  never betray him:
His Sea that his being fulfils?
So and no otherwise-so and no otherwise — hillmen desire
  their Hills.

Christmas

⟹ 1954 ⟸

SIR JOHN BETJEMAN

H IS TWO POEMS 'Christmas' and 'A Subaltern's Love-song'
alone must surely have earned John Betjeman his knighthood
and Poet Laureateship. *The Times* dubbed him 'by appointment:
Teddy Bear to the nation'.

> The bells of waiting Advent ring,
>   The Tortoise stove is lit again
> And lamp-oil light across the night
>   Has caught the streaks of winter rain
> In many a stained-glass window sheen
> From Crimson Lake to Hooker's Green.
>
> The holly in the windy hedge
>   And round the Manor House the yew
> Will soon be stripped to deck the ledge,
>   The altar, font and arch and pew,
> So that the villagers can say
> 'The church looks nice' on Christmas Day.
>
> Provincial public houses blaze
>   And Corporation tramcars clang,
> On lighted tenements I gaze,
>   Where paper decorations hang,
> And bunting in the red Town Hall
> Says 'Merry Christmas to you all.'

And London shops on Christmas Eve
    Are strung with silver bells and flowers
As hurrying clerks the City leave
    To pigeon-haunted classic towers,
And marbled clouds go scudding by
The many-steepled London sky.

And girls in slacks remember Dad,
    And oafish louts remember Mum,
And sleepless children's hearts are glad,
    And Christmas-morning bells say 'Come!'
Even to shining ones who dwell
Safe in the Dorchester Hotel.

And is it true? And is it true,
    This most tremendous tale of all,
Seen in a stained-glass window's hue,
    A Baby in an ox's stall?
The Maker of the stars and sea
Become a Child on earth for me?

And is it true? For if it is,
    No loving fingers tying strings
Around those tissued fripperies,
    The sweet and silly Christmas things,
Bath salts and inexpensive scent
And hideous tie so kindly meant,

No love that in a family dwells,
    No carolling in frosty air,
Nor all the steeple-shaking bells
    Can with this single Truth compare —
That God was Man in Palestine
And lives to-day in Bread and Wine.

5

THE UNDERDOG

P ERHAPS WE ENGLISH do think of ourselves as an
underdog: an unnoticed, geographically obscure island
on the fringes of things that time and again, in the words
of Pitt the Younger, saves the world by both her exertions
and her example.

And perhaps also our unique history, our isolation, our
waves of immigration, our industrial head start and our
ancient freedoms have allowed the underdog to flourish
here as nowhere else.

Whatever the reason, sympathy for the underdog is
one of our great national characteristics. Facing hopeless
odds, whether it be ourselves or anyone else, seems to
stir something within us. (I wonder whether this might
explain our love of pets?) Each one of the following poems
has an underdog of one sort or another as its subject.

Lines to a Don

—⇒ 1910 ⇐—

HILAIRE BELLOC

MY PATERNAL GRANDMOTHER, who was French, used to say that all the most interesting people had at least one foreign grandparent. Certainly an association or close relationship with another country seems to help people appreciate their own. Winston Churchill, whose mother was American, is a case in point, as was Hilaire Belloc, who was born in France in 1870.

After Oxford Belloc served as the Liberal MP for Salford from 1906 to 1910. As a Catholic he defied the electorate with the magnificent statement: 'I am a Catholic. As far as possible I go to Mass every day. If you reject me on account of my religion, I shall thank God that he has spared me the indignity of being your representative.'

Belloc wrote verse, essays, biographies, and travel and history books and was also a journalist and editor. He once said, 'I'm tired of love: I'm still more tired of rhyme but money gives me pleasure all the time.'

> Remote and ineffectual Don
> That dared attack my Chesterton,
> With that poor weapon, half-impelled,
> Unlearnt, unsteady, hardly held,
> Unworthy for a tilt with men —
> Your quavering and corroded pen;
> Don poor at Bed and worse at Table,
> Don pinched, Don starved, Don miserable;
> Don stuttering, Don with roving eyes,
> Don nervous, Don of crudities;
> Don clerical, Don ordinary,
> Don self-absorbed and solitary;
> Don here-and-there, Don epileptic;

Don puffed and empty, Don dyspeptic;
Don middle-class, Don sycophantic,
Don dull, Don brutish, Don pedantic,
Don hypocritical, Don bad,
Don furtive, Don three-quarters mad;
Don (since a man must make an end),
Don that shall never be my friend.

Don different from those regal Dons!
With hearts of gold and lungs of bronze,
Who shout and bang and roar and bawl
The Absolute across the hall,
Or sail in amply billowing gown
Enormous through the Sacred Town,
Bearing from College to their homes
Deep cargoes of gigantic tomes;
Dons admirable! Dons of Might!
Uprising on my inward sight
Compact of ancient tales, and port
And sleep — and learning of a sort.
Dons English, worthy of the land;
Dons rooted; Dons that understand.
Good Dons perpetual that remain
A landmark, walling in the plain —
The horizon of my memories
Like large and comfortable trees.

Don very much apart from these,
Thou scapegoat Don, thou Don devoted,
Don to thine own damnation quoted,
Perplexed to find thy trivial name
Reared in my verse to lasting shame.
Don dreadful, rasping Don and wearing,
Repulsive Don — Don past all bearing.

Don of the cold and doubtful breath,
Don despicable, Don of death;
Don nasty, skimpy, silent, level;
Don evil; Don that serves the devil.
Don ugly—that makes fifty lines.
There is a Canon which confines
A Rhymed Octosyllabic Curse
If written in Iambic Verse
To fifty lines. I never cut;
I far prefer to end it — but
Believe me I shall soon return.
My fires are banked, but still they burn
To write some more about the Don
That dared attack my Chesterton.

Epitaph on an Army of Mercenaries
1915

A. E. HOUSMAN

A. E. HOUSMAN is best known for his collection of poems *A Shropshire Lad*, which he published at his own expense in 1896. The book attracted little attention initially but it became hugely popular during the First World War.

Born in Worcestershire in 1859, Housman went to Oxford, where, though a brilliant scholar, he somehow managed to fail his finals. He became a clerk in a patent office for ten years, still pursuing his classical studies and periodically publishing articles. His scholarship was finally recognised with his appointment to University College London, as professor of Latin in 1892. In 1911 he became professor of Latin at Cambridge.

The 'mercenaries' referred to in this poem are the British Expeditionary Force under General French, British Army regulars who were sent out to hold up the Germans at the beginning of the First World War. They earned the nickname the 'Old Contemptibles' from the Kaiser's order to his generals on 19 August 1914: 'It is my Royal and Imperial command that you exterminate the treacherous English and walk over General French's contemptible little army.'

These, in the day when heaven was falling,
　　The hour when earth's foundations fled,
Followed their mercenary calling,
　　And took their wages, and are dead.

Their shoulders held the sky suspended;
　　They stood, and earth's foundations stay;
What God abandoned, these defended,
　　And saved the sum of things for pay.

From The Ballad of Reading Gaol
⟹ 1897 ⟸
OSCAR WILDE

OSCAR WILDE COINED the phrase 'nothing succeeds like excess' and throughout his life he went out of his way to arouse the hostility of those he considered stuffy and pedestrian. He was born in Dublin in 1854 and went to Trinity College and then Oxford, where he was a brilliant classical scholar and taunted his contemporaries by incidents like his refusal to play cricket on the grounds that 'it requires one to assume such indecent postures'. His claim to be a proponent of 'art for art's sake' was deemed almost equally shocking. He undertook a hugely successful lecture tour in America and wrote novels and plays, publishing his masterpiece, *The Importance of Being Earnest*, in 1895.

He was imprisoned for homosexual offences in 1895, declaring as he was bundled through the rain into a prison transport that, 'If this is the way Queen Victoria treats her prisoners, she doesn't deserve to have any.'

Released from prison in 1897, Wilde went into exile in France, where he wrote *The Ballad of Reading Gaol*. He died in 1900 in squalid rented Parisian digs after waving at the wallpaper and saying, 'One of us must go.'

> He did not wear his scarlet coat,
>   For blood and wine are red,
> And blood and wine were on his hands
>   When they found him with the dead,
> The poor dead woman whom he loved,
>   And murdered in her bed.

He walked amongst the Trial Men
    In a suit of shabby grey;
A cricket cap was on his head,
    And his step seemed light and gay;
But I never saw a man who looked
    So wistfully at the day.

I never saw a man who looked
    With such a wistful eye
Upon that little tent of blue
    Which prisoners call the sky,
And at every drifting cloud that went
    With sails of silver by.

I walked, with other souls in pain,
    Within another ring,
And was wondering if the man had done
    A great or little thing,
When a voice behind me whispered low,
    'That fellow's got to swing.'

The Mower
1979
PHILIP LARKIN

LIBRARIANS ARE SUPPOSED to be dull and, indeed, in photographs Philip Larkin seems to fit the stereotype, always looking thoroughly staid and straightforward. Yet his poetry teems with agonising sentiment and insight. From the utterly mundane and typically English activity of mowing the lawn he conjures up this wonderful poem.

Larkin is obsessed with time and with the idea that it is running out, for him and the things he loves. But from this dread he extracts the lovely final injunction.

> The mower stalled, twice; kneeling, I found
> A hedgehog jammed up against the blades,
> Killed. It had been in the long grass.
>
> I had seen it before, and even fed it, once.
> Now I had mauled its unobtrusive world
> Unmendably. Burial was no help:
>
> Next morning I got up and it did not.
> The first day after a death, the new absence
> Is always the same; we should be careful
>
> Of each other, we should be kind
> While there is still time.

Sonnet XXIX

1595

WILLIAM SHAKESPEARE

A FRIEND OF MINE at university studying English said he could only really 'get' Shakespeare if he read it out loud in a silly voice. This he did for an entire term until the Dean 'popped round to check everything was ok'. Even his implausible Morningside accent could not detract from the phrases 'beweeping my outcast state', 'bootless cries', 'a lark at break of day arising' and 'singing hymns at heaven's gate'.

When in disgrace with fortune and men's eyes,
    I all alone beweep my outcast state,
And trouble deaf heaven with my bootless cries,
    And look upon myself, and curse my fate,
Wishing me like to one more rich in hope,
    Featured like him, like him with friends possessed,
Desiring this man's art and that man's scope,
    With what I most enjoy contented least;
Yet in these thoughts myself almost despising,
    Haply I think on thee, and then my state,
Like to the lark at break of day arising
    From sullen earth, sings hymns at heaven's gate;
      For thy sweet love remembered such wealth brings
      That then I scorn to change my state with Kings.

The Donkey
1900

G. K. Chesterton

THE JOURNALIST G. K. Chesterton always took the side of the underdog against big business, bureaucracy and technology. Like his fictional character Father Brown, a quiet, bumbling, East Anglian priest-come-detective, he was interested in everything, once saying, 'Is ditch water dull? Naturalists with microscopes have told me that it teems with quiet fun.' Much of his writing delights in England and the English.

He was born in London in 1874, educated at St Paul's and converted to Roman Catholicism in 1922. Famously overweight, when asked towards the end of his life if he did not find his size a handicap, he insisted it did have its consolations: 'Just the other day in London I enjoyed the pleasure of accommodating three young ladies at the same time – I gave them my seat on the underground.'

> When fishes flew and forests walked
>   And figs grew upon thorn,
> Some moment when the moon was blood
>   Then surely I was born;
>
> With monstrous head and sickening cry
>   And ears like errant wings,
> The devil's walking parody
>   On all four-footed things.
>
> The tattered outlaw of the earth
>   Of ancient crooked will;
> Starve, scourge, deride me: I am dumb
>   I keep my secret still.

Fools! For I also had my hour;
    One far fierce hour and sweet:
There was a shout about my ears,
    And palms before my feet.

Poor Puggy-Wug
1936

WINSTON CHURCHILL

DESPITE SAVING THE free world, winning the Nobel Prize, turning down a dukedom, being a war correspondent, Lieutenant Colonel, Under Secretary of State for the Colonies, President of the Board of Trade, Home Secretary, First Lord of the Admiralty, Secretary of State for War, Chancellor of the Exchequer and Prime Minister with a passion for painting, bricklaying and history, Winston Churchill is not known for his poetry. He did love pigs, though – and pugs.

William of Orange first brought pugs to England in the seventeenth century and they became the favoured royal dog until the abdication of Edward VIII. According to legend, William the Silent of Holland (1533–84), having been sent a consignment of table dogs (for eating) from some Dutch traders in the East Indies, had a basket of puppies awaiting preparation on campaign with him. Their yapping alerted the Dutch to the approach of the Spanish, thus saving Holland. The pugs were instantly elevated from the larder to the throne room.

> Oh, what is the matter with poor Puggy-wug?
> Pet him and kiss him and give him a hug.
> Run and fetch him a suitable drug.
> Wrap him up tenderly, all in a rug.
> That is the way to cure poor Puggy-wug.

Church Going

=➡ 1955 ⇐=

PHILIP LARKIN

THERE IS AN undeniable hopelessness about Philip Larkin, hope-lessness tempered with resignation. But despite questions like 'what are days for? Days are where we live', frequent suggestions of the futility of everything and the powerlessness of modern man, he is 'forever surprising a hunger in himself', and an 'endearing awkward reverence'.

Once I am sure there's nothing going on
I step inside, letting the door thud shut.
Another church: matting, seats, and stone,
And little books; sprawlings of flowers, cut
For Sunday, brownish now; some brass and stuff
Up at the holy end; the small neat organ;
And a tense, musty, unignorable silence,
Brewed God knows how long. Hatless, I take off
My cycle-clips in awkward reverence,

Move forward, run my hand around the font.
From where I stand, the roof looks almost new —
Cleaned, or restored? Someone would know: I don't.
Mounting the lectern, I peruse a few
Hectoring large-scale verses, and pronounce
'Here endeth' much more loudly than I'd meant.
The echoes snigger briefly. Back at the door
I sign the book, donate an Irish sixpence,
Reflect the place was not worth stopping for.

Yet stop I did: in fact I often do,
And always end much at a loss like this,
Wondering what to look for; wondering, too,

When churches fall completely out of use
What we shall turn them into, if we shall keep
A few cathedrals chronically on show,
Their parchment, plate, and pyx in locked cases,
And let the rest rent-free to rain and sheep.
Shall we avoid them as unlucky places?

Or, after dark, will dubious women come
To make their children touch a particular stone;
Pick simples for a cancer; or on some
Advised night see walking a dead one?
Power of some sort or other will go on
In games, in riddles, seemingly at random;
But superstition, like belief, must die,
And what remains when disbelief has gone?
Grass, weedy pavement, brambles, buttress, sky,

A shape less recognisable each week,
A purpose more obscure. I wonder who
Will be the last, the very last, to seek
This place for what it was; one of the crew
That tap and jot and know what rood-lofts were?
Some ruin-bibber, randy for antique,
Or Christmas-addict, counting on a whiff
Of gown-and-bands and organ-pipes and myrrh?
Or will he be my representative,

Bored, uninformed, knowing the ghostly silt
Dispersed, yet tending to this cross of ground
Through suburb scrub because it held unspilt
So long and equably what since is found
Only in separation — marriage, and birth,
And death, and thoughts of these — for whom was built

This special shell? For, though I've no idea
What this accoutred frowsty barn is worth,
It pleases me to stand in silence here;

A serious house on serious earth it is,
In whose blent air all our compulsions meet,
Are recognised, and robed as destinies.
And that much never can be obsolete,
Since someone will forever be surprising
A hunger in himself to be more serious,
And gravitating with it to this ground,
Which, he once heard, was proper to grow wise in,
If only that so many dead lie round.

6

PRAYER

THIS CHAPTER CONSISTS of poems that also happen to be prayers, defined by the Oxford English Dictionary as 'devout supplications to God'. Some perhaps do not quite fit this definition but I include them on the basis that the poets are reflecting or meditating upon God and in some way communing with Him. One is a psalm, the word being derived from the Greek word psallo, meaning 'twang', the twang of a harp string, an instrument upon which the great psalmist David was particularly adept.

From Jubilate Agno
⟹ 1760 ⟸

CHRISTOPHER SMART

CHRISTOPHER SMART WAS born in Kent in 1722 and brought up in Durham. He was educated at Cambridge, where he was made a fellow of Pembroke College in 1745. Four years later he went to London to become a journalist.

In 1756 he felt an 'increasing compulsion to public prayer' and his religious mania became so intense that he was admitted to a hospital for the insane in 1757. He was transferred to a private lunatic asylum in Bethnal Green and he stayed there for the next six years. It was here that he wrote this poem, 'Jubilate Agno' ('Rejoice the Lamb'), though it was not published until 1939.

On his release from the asylum he wrote his most famous poem, 'A Song to David', according to his own rather complicated mathematical criteria, which Browning compared to a great cathedral. He died in debtors' prison in 1771.

Surprisingly, considering his interest in science and cats, Smart had a particular loathing for his cat-loving Cambridge contemporary Sir Isaac Newton, who invented the cat flap.

For I will consider my Cat Jeoffry.
For he is the servant of the Living God duly and daily serving him.
For at the first glance of the glory of God in the East he
worships in his way.
For this is done by wreathing his body seven times round with
elegant quickness.
For then he leaps up to catch the musk, which is the blessing of
God upon his prayer.
For he rolls upon prank to work it in.
For having done duty and received blessing he begins to
consider himself.
For this he performs in ten degrees.

For first he looks upon his forepaws to see if they are clean.

For secondly he kicks up behind to clear away there.

For thirdly he works it upon stretch with the forepaws extended.

For fourthly he sharpens his paws by wood.

For fifthly he washes himself.

For sixthly he rolls upon wash.

For seventhly he fleas himself, that he may not be interrupted upon the beat.

For eighthly he rubs himself against a post.

For ninthly he looks up for his instructions.

For tenthly he goes in quest of food.

For having consider'd God and himself he will consider his neighbour.

For if he meets another cat he will kiss her in kindness.

For when he takes his prey he plays with it to give it a chance.

For one mouse in seven escapes by his dallying.

For when his day's work is done his business more properly begins.

For he keeps the Lord's watch in the night against the adversary.

For he counteracts the powers of darkness by his electrical skin and glaring eyes.

For he counteracts the Devil, who is death, by brisking about the life.

For in his morning orisons he loves the sun and the sun loves him.

For he is of the tribe of Tiger.

For the Cherub Cat is a term of the Angel Tiger.

For he has the subtlety and hissing of a serpent, which in goodness he suppresses.

For he will not do destruction, if he is well-fed, neither will he spit without provocation.

For he purrs in thankfulness, when God tells him he's a good Cat.

For he is an instrument for the children to learn benevolence upon.

For every house is incompleat without him and a blessing is lacking in the spirit.

For the Lord commanded Moses concerning the cats at the
   departure of the Children of Israel from Egypt.

For every family had one cat at least in the bag.

For the English Cats are the best in Europe.

For he is the cleanest in the use of his forepaws of any
   quadrupede.

For the dexterity of his defence is an instance of the love of God
   to him exceedingly.

For he is the quickest to his mark of any creature.

For he is tenacious of his point.

For he is a mixture of gravity and waggery.

For he knows that God is his Saviour.

For there is nothing sweeter than his peace even at rest.

For there is nothing brisker than his life when in motion.

For he is of the Lord's poor and so indeed is he called by
   benevolence perpetually — Poor Jeoffry! poor Jeoffry! the
   rat has bit thy throat.

For I bless the name of the Lord Jesus that Jeoffry is better.

For the divine spirit comes about his body to sustain it in
   compleat cat.

For his tongue is exceeding pure so that it has in purity what it
   wants in musick.

For he is docile and can learn certain things.

For he can set up with gravity, which is patience upon
   approbation.

For he can fetch and carry, which is patience in employment.

For he can jump over a stick, which is patience upon proof
   positive.

For he can spraggle upon waggle at the word of command.

For he can jump from an eminence into his master's bosom.

For he can catch the cork and toss it again.

For he is hated by the hypocrite and miser.

For the former is afraid of detection.

For the latter refuses the charge.

For he camels his back to bear the first notion of business.
For he is good to think on, if a man would express himself neatly.
For he was made a great figure in Egypt for his signal services.
For he killed the Ichneumon-rat very pernicious by land.
For his ears are so acute that they sting again.
For from this proceeds the passing quickness of his attention.
For by stroking of him I have found out electricity.
For I perceived God's light about him both wax and fire.
For the Electrical fire is the spiritual substance, which God sends
    from heaven to sustain the bodies both of man and beast.
For God has blessed him in the variety of his movements.
For, tho' he cannot fly, he is an excellent clamberer.
For his motions upon the face of the earth are more than any
    other quadrupede.
For he can tread to all the measures upon the musick.
For he can swim for life.
For he can creep.

Pied Beauty
1877
GERARD MANLEY HOPKINS

BLAKE'S 'THE TIGER', Smart's 'Jubilate Agno' and this poem, 'Pied Beauty', are all hymns in praise of the Creator and His creation. Reciting 'Pied Beauty' out loud while walking, especially in Essex, where 'the skies of couple-colour as a brinded cow' are often breathtaking, induces a kind of daze-like euphoria.

> Glory be to God for dappled things —
>   For skies of couple-colour as a brinded cow;
>   For rose-moles all in stipple upon trout that swim;
> Fresh-firecoal chestnut-falls, finches' wings;
>   Landscape plotted and pieced — fold, fallow and plough;
>   And all trades, their gear and tackle and trim.
>
> All things counter, original, spare, strange;
>   Whatever is fickle, freckled (who knows how?)
>   With swift, slow; sweet, sour; adazzle, dim;
> He fathers-forth whose beauty is past change:
>
> Praise him.

Love (III)

───➤ 1630 ⇐───

GEORGE HERBERT

GEORGE HERBERT WAS born in Montgomery Castle in Wales in 1593 into a rather grand local family. His father died when he was three. His mother was a friend and patron of the poet John Donne.

He was educated at Westminster, then Cambridge, where he was Reader in Rhetoric and Public Orator from 1619 to 1627, and frequently at court. In 1624 he represented Montgomery in parliament. He was obliged to take holy orders within seven years of becoming a fellow and was ordained in 1626.

When he became Rector of Bemerton in Wiltshire in 1630, having become gradually disillusioned with life at the centre of things, he abandoned London life completely. He restored a church at his own expense, got married, adopted two children and quietly acquired a reputation for simple piety and energetic, practical charity.

It is typical of his humility that he sent his poems to a friend when he realised he was dying of consumption, aged 39, with instructions that they should be published if it was thought that they 'might turn to the advantage of any dejected soul'; otherwise they should be burnt.

Love bade me welcome; yet my soul drew back,
        Guilty of dust and
sin.
But quick-eyed Love, observing me grow slack
        From my first
entrance in,
Drew nearer to me, sweetly questioning,
        If I lacked anything.

'A guest,' I answered, 'worthy to be here.'
                    Love said, 'You shall
be he.'
'I the unkind, ungrateful? Ah my dear,
                    I cannot look on
thee.'
Love took my hand, and smiling did reply,
                    'Who made the eyes
but I?'

Truth, Lord, but I have marred them: let my shame
                    Go where it doth
deserve.'
'And know you not,' says Love, 'who bore the blame?'
                    'My dear, then I will
serve.'
'You must sit down,' says Love, 'and taste my meat.'
                    So I did sit and eat.

Prayer
⟹ 1622 ⟸

John Donne

DESPITE THE FACT that his brother died in prison, having been arrested for harbouring a Catholic priest, John Donne nevertheless described the different Christian Churches of his time as 'all rays of the same sun'. He believed that the Anglican church could swamp extremists on both sides with liberality and love.

My wife loves this prayer.

> Bring us, O Lord God, at our last awakening
> Into the house and gate of heaven,
> To enter into that gate and dwell in that house,
> Where there shall be no darkness
> Nor dazzling but one equal light;
> No noise nor silence,
> But one equal music;
> No hopes nor fears,
> But one equal possession;
> No ends nor beginnings,
> But one equal eternity,
> Within the habitations of thy Glory
> And thy dominion, world without end.
> Amen

A Hymn to God the Father
1623

JOHN DONNE

K ING JAMES I, to whom Donne was Royal Chaplain, said
'Doctor Donne's verses are like the Peace of God: they pass
all understanding.' Donne was indeed one of the great intellectual
preachers of James's reign. Here he plays on the words 'Donne'
and 'done' and explores the notions of his own sin and salvation.

> Wilt thou forgive that sin where I begun,
>   Which is my sin, though it were done before?
> Wilt thou forgive those sins through which I run,
>   And do them still, though still I do deplore?
>   When thou hast done, thou hast not done,
>   For I have more.
>
> Wilt thou forgive that sin by which I won
>   Others to sin? and made my sin their door?
> Wilt thou forgive that sin which I did shun
>   A year or two, but wallowed in a score?
>   When thou hast done, thou hast not done,
>   For I have more.
>
> I have a sin of fear, that when I have spun
>   My last thread, I shall perish on the shore;
> Swear by thyself, that at my death thy Sun
>   Shall shine as it shines now, and heretofore;
>   And, having done that, thou hast done,
>   I have no more.

Psalm 23

═══ ➤ 1650 ═══

SCOTTISH METRICAL VERSION

BEFORE WE MARRIED, my wife was a nurse at the London Hospital. I was particularly shocked at the calm and tenderness with which she and her colleagues coped with pain and death. Patients would often ask the nurses to say prayers or psalms with them when they were frightened, or even dying, the 23rd Psalm more than any other.

Sheep and shepherds are, of course, common Christian images but perhaps for the English, who were once outnumbered six to one by the national flock, which then constituted 'half the wealth of England', they have a special place.

> The Lord's my Shepherd, I'll not want:
>   He maketh me down to lie
> In pastures green; He leadeth me
>   The quiet waters by.
>
> My soul He doth restore again,
>   And me to walk doth make
> Within the paths of righteousness,
>   E'en for His own Name's sake.
>
> Yea, though I walk in death's dark vale,
>   Yet will I fear none ill;
> For Thou art with me, and Thy rod
>   And staff me comfort still.
>
> My table Thou hast furnishèd
>   In presence of my foes;
> My head Thou dost with oil anoint,
>   And my cup overflows.

Goodness and mercy all my life
    Shall surely follow me;
And in God's house for evermore
    My dwelling-place shall be.

The Collar
1630

GEORGE HERBERT

GEORGE HERBERT SAID his poetry painted 'a picture of the many spiritual conflicts that have passed betwixt God and my soul, before I could subject mine before the will of Jesus my Master'.

I struck the board, and cried, 'No more!
                    I
will abroad.
    What? shall I ever sigh and pine?
My lines and life are free; free as the road,
        Loose as the wind, as large as store.
                Shall I be still in suit?
        Have I no harvest but a thorn
        To let me blood, and not restore
    What I have lost with cordial fruit?
                        Sure
there was wine
Before my sighs did dry it: there was corn
            Before my tears did drown it.
        Is the year only lost to me?
            Have I no bays to crown it?
No flowers, no garlands gay? all blasted?
                    All
wasted?
    No so, my heart: but there is fruit,
                And
thou hast hands.
    Recover all thy sigh-blown age
On double pleasures: leave thy cold dispute

Of what is fit and not. Forsake thy cage,
                    Thy
rope of sands,
Which petty thoughts have made, and made to thee
    Good cable, to enforce and draw,
                    And
be thy law,
    While thou didst wink and wouldst not see.
                    Away;
take heed:
                    I
will abroad.
Call in thy death's head there: tie up thy fears;
                    He
that forbears
            To suit and serve his need,

Deserves his load.'
But as I raved and grew more fierce and wild
                    At
every word,
    Methought I heard one calling, 'Child!'
            And I replied, 'My Lord'.

Recessional (A Victorian Ode)
1897

RUDYARD KIPLING

IT IS STILL fashionable to dismiss Kipling's poetry as a relic of Empire but this is nothing new for he always attracted a fair amount of flack. Henry James described him as an 'infant monster'. Yet this poem, written for Queen Victoria's Jubilee Day in 1897, was hailed at the time for catching the mood of the moment. It doesn't seem such a bad mood, praying for a humble and contrite heart, for the rule of law, the guidance of God and protection against the intoxication of power. By 'lesser breeds without the Law' Kipling meant the Germans, who were indeed to deploy 'reeking tube and iron shard' with such devastating effect in the First World War.

> God of our fathers, known of old,
>   Lord of our far-flung battle-line,
> Beneath whose awful Hand we hold
>   Dominion over palm and pine —
> Lord God of Hosts, be with us yet,
> Lest we forget — lest we forget!
>
> The tumult and the shouting dies;
>   The Captains and the Kings depart:
> Still stands Thine ancient sacrifice,
>   An humble and a contrite heart.
> Lord God of Hosts, be with us yet,
> Lest we forget — lest we forget!

Far-called, our navies melt away;
    On dune and headland sinks the fire:
Lo, all our pomp of yesterday
    Is one with Nineveh and Tyre!
Judge of the Nations, spare us yet,
Lest we forget — lest we forget!

If, drunk with sight of power, we loose
    Wild tongues that have not Thee in awe,
Such boasting as the Gentiles use,
    Or lesser breeds without the Law —
Lord God of Hosts, be with us yet,
Lest we forget — lest we forget!

For heathen heart that puts her trust
    In reeking tube and iron shard,
All valiant dust that builds on dust,
    And guarding, calls not Thee to guard,
For frantic boast and foolish word —
Thy Mercy on Thy People, Lord!

Amen.

'Give me my scallop-shell of quiet' from
The Passionate Man's Pilgrimage

—— 1604 ——

SIR WALTER RALEIGH

IN HIS WONDERFUL anthology *Other Men's Flowers*, Field Marshal Earl Wavell GCB, GCSI, GCIE, CMG, MC, compares 'Jerusalem' by Blake, the man of peace, with its talk of arrows, swords, spears, chariots and shields with this poem by Sir Walter Raleigh, the man of war, with its talk of shells of quiet, staffs of faith and bottles of salvation.

Born in Devon and educated at Oxford, Raleigh was indeed a man of war. Having fought in France and Ireland he arrived at Queen Elizabeth I's court and was knighted in 1584. The Queen was so jealous of the attentions he was paying to one of her maids of honour that he was imprisoned in the tower for seducing a lady-in-waiting in 1592. He married that same maid of honour/lady-in-waiting, Elizabeth Throgmorton, when he was released a year later.

He explored the Caribbean, led expeditions against Spain, founded Virginia and introduced potatoes and tobacco into England.

1603 found him in prison again, as James I sought to placate the Spanish, and he was not released until 1616, when he set sail for South America on his second expedition to search the Orinoco for gold. He was sentenced to death on a charge of conspiracy on his return to England, having failed to bring back any treasure and burnt a Spanish settlement. He was executed in 1618 at Old Palace Yard, Westminster. He was 66.

Give me my scallop-shell of quiet,
My staff of faith to walk upon,
My scrip of joy, immortal diet,
My bottle of salvation,
My gown of glory, hope's true gage,
And thus I'll take my pilgrimage.

7

MAGIC

GOOD ESSEX CHILDREN used to be taught to sing whenever we crossed the county boundary, into Suffolk, for instance, for good luck. I understand that this superstition dates back to Saxon times when the counties were independent kingdoms. In those days the only people, other than the nobility, allowed to move around freely were the travelling bards or minstrels, who were an essential source of news and entertainment.

The idea of those Dark Age bards singing in the firelight of ancient village halls, where the music of the words and the fantastic tales kept entire communities on the edge of their seats, has forged for me an inextricable link between magic and poetry.

The Old Ships
1915

JAMES ELROY FLECKER

IF EVERYONE WHO worked for the Edwardian Consular Service
had an imagination like James Elroy Flecker then what an amazing
organisation it must have been. The timeless and magical adventure of trade and the beauty of the dawn are two recurring themes
in his poetry.

I have seen old ships sail like swans asleep
Beyond the village which men still call Tyre,
With leaden age o'ercargoed, dipping deep
For Famagusta and the hidden sun
That rings black Cyprus with a lake of fire;
And all those ships were certainly so old —
Who knows how oft with squat and noisy gun,
Questing brown slaves or Syrian oranges,
The pirate Genoese
Hell-raked them till they rolled
Blood, water, fruit and corpses up the hold.
But now through friendly seas they softly run,
Painted the mid-sea blue or shore-sea green,
Still patterned with the vine and grapes in gold.

But I have seen,
Pointing her shapely shadows from the dawn
And image tumbled on a rose-swept bay,
A drowsy ship of some yet older day;
And, wonder's breath indrawn,
Thought I — who knows — who knows — but in that same
(Fished up beyond Aeaea, patched up new
  — Stern painted brighter blue —)
That talkative, bald-headed seaman came

(Twelve patient comrades sweating at the oar)
From Troy's doom-crimson shore,
And with great lies about his wooden horse
Set the crew laughing, and forgot his course.

It was so old a ship — who knows, who knows?
— And yet so beautiful, I watched in vain
To see the mast burst open with a rose,
And the whole deck put on its leaves again.

Kubla Khan
1798

Samuel Taylor Coleridge

SAMUEL TAYLOR COLERIDGE was born in 1772, the youngest son of the vicar of Ottery St Mary in Devon. On the death of his father, he was sent away to a school in London and went on to Cambridge, where the end of a love affair prompted him to enlist in the army under the false name of Comberbache. His brother secured his release on the grounds that his French revolutionary politics proved he was insane and he returned to Cambridge for a while, though he never took his degree.

He met the poet Robert Southey on a walking tour and they planned to set up a 'democratical commune' in New England. He married Southey's sister-in-law and considered becoming a Unitarian minister. His friendship with Wordsworth, who he met in 1797, had a profound influence on both their work for at least 14 years. Coleridge also spent time in Germany and, as his marriage failed, became disastrously addicted to opium. He took the position of secretary to the Governor of wartime Malta for two years and afterwards travelled in Italy.

In 1814 he re-found his Christian faith, publicly admitted his addiction to opium and took steps to tackle it. He was a mesmerising lecturer – Charles Lamb described him as 'a slightly damaged archangel' – and he believed science was the enemy of poetry, insisting that it would take the souls of 500 Isaac Newtons to make one Shakespeare or Milton.

Coleridge wrote 'Kubla Khan' in the early stages of his drug addiction, 'eagerly writing the lines' after awaking from an opium-fuelled dream, only to be interrupted by a 'person on business from Porlock'.

In Xanadu did Kubla Khan
    A stately pleasure-dome decree:
Where Alph, the sacred river, ran
Through caverns measureless to man
    Down to a sunless sea.
    So twice five miles of fertile ground
    With walls and towers were girdled round:
And there were gardens bright with sinuous rills,
Where blossomed many an incense-bearing tree;
And here were forests ancient as the hills,
Enfolding sunny spots of greenery.

But O! that deep romantic chasm which slanted
Down the green hill athwart a cedarn cover!
A savage place! as holy and enchanted
As e'er beneath a waning moon was haunted
By woman wailing for her demon-lover!
And from this chasm, with ceaseless turmoil seething,
As if this earth in fast thick pants were breathing,
A mighty fountain momently was forced:
Amid whose swift half-intermitted burst
Huge fragments vaulted like rebounding hail,
Or chaffy grain beneath the thresher's flail:
And 'mid these dancing rocks at once and ever
It flung up momently the sacred river.
Five miles meandering with a mazy motion
Through wood and dale the sacred river ran,
Then reached the caverns measureless to man,
And sank in tumult to a lifeless ocean:
And 'mid this tumult Kubla heard from far
Ancestral voices prophesying war!

The shadow of the dome of pleasure
    Floated midway on the waves;
Where was heard the mingled measure
    From the fountain and the caves.
It was a miracle of rare device,
A sunny pleasure-dome with caves of ice!

A damsel with a dulcimer
    In a vision once I saw:
It was an Abyssinian maid,
    And on her dulcimer she played,
Singing of Mount Abora.
Could I revive within me
Her symphony and song,
To such a deep delight 'twould win me,
That with music loud and long,
I would build that dome in air,
That sunny dome! those caves of ice!
And all who heard should see them there,
And all should cry, 'Beware! Beware!
His flashing eyes, his floating hair!
Weave a circle round him thrice,
    And close your eyes with holy dread,
    For he on honey-dew hath fed,
And drunk the milk of Paradise.'

Ozymandias
⟹ 1819 ⟸
PERCY BYSSHE SHELLEY

SHELLEY WAS BORN in Sussex in 1792. He went to Eton and then Oxford, from where he was sent down after publishing a pamphlet entitled 'The Necessity of Atheism'. In 1811 he eloped with the 16-year-old Harriet Westbrook. They had two children but Shelley left her for Mary Wollstonecraft Godwin (the future author of *Frankenstein*), whom he married after his first wife's suicide in 1816. He travelled with Byron to Switzerland and moved on to Italy in 1818. He was drowned there in 1822, having recklessly taken out his new yacht, adapted for speed, in a terrible storm.

I met a traveller from an antique land
Who said: Two vast and trunkless legs of stone
Stand in the desert . . . Near them, on the sand,
Half sunk, a shattered visage lies, whose frown,
And wrinkled lip, and sneer of cold command,
Tell that its sculptor well those passions read
Which yet survive, stamped on these lifeless things,
The hand that mocked them, and the heart that fed:
And on the pedestal these words appear:
'My name is Ozymandias, King of Kings:
Look on my works, ye Mighty, and despair!'
Nothing beside remains. Round the decay
Of that colossal wreck, boundless and bare
The lone and level sands stretch far away.

The Listeners

1912

WALTER DE LA MARE

WALTER DE LA MARE was born in Kent in 1873 and educated at St Paul's Choir School. For 20 years, from the age of 16 to 36, he worked for an oil company. He wrote poetry, novels and short stories for adults and children, and essays and commentaries. He became a Companion of Honour in 1948 and was awarded the Order of Merit in 1953. He died in 1956 and is buried in St Paul's Cathedral.

'Is there anybody there?' said the Traveller,
    Knocking on the moonlit door;
And his horse in the silence champed the grasses
    Of the forest's ferny floor:
And a bird flew up out of the turret,
    Above the Traveller's head:
And he smote upon the door again a second time;
    'Is there anybody there?' he said.
But no one descended to the Traveller;
    No head from the leaf-fringed sill
Leaned over and looked into his grey eyes,
    Where he stood perplexed and still.
But only a host of phantom listeners
    That dwelt in the lone house then
Stood listening in the quiet of the moonlight
    To that voice from the world of men:
Stood thronging the faint moonbeams on the dark stair,
    That goes down to the empty hall,
Hearkening in an air stirred and shaken
    By the lonely Traveller's call.
And he felt in his heart their strangeness,
    Their stillness answering his cry,

While his horse moved, cropping the dark turf,
    'Neath the starred and leafy sky;
For he suddenly smote the door, even
    Louder, and lifted his head:—
'Tell them I came, and no one answered,
    That I kept my word,' he said.
Never the least stir made the listeners,
    Though every word he spake
Fell echoing through the shadowiness of the still house
    From the one man left awake:
Ay, they heard his foot upon the stirrup,
    And the sound of iron on stone,
And how the silence surged softly backward,
    When the plunging hoofs were gone.

All That's Past

1912

WALTER DE LA MARE

Very old are the woods;
    And the buds that break
Out of the brier's boughs,
    When March winds wake,
So old with their beauty are –
    Oh, no man knows
Through what wild centuries
    Roves back the rose.

Very old are the brooks;
    And the rills that rise
Where snow sleeps cold beneath
    The azure skies
Sing such a history
    Of come and gone,
Their every drop is as wise
    As Solomon.

Very old are we men;
    Our dreams are tales
Told in dim Eden
    By Eve's nightingales;
We wake and whisper awhile,
    But, the day gone by,
Silence and sleep like fields
    Of amaranth lie.

Jabberwocky
— 1872 —

LEWIS CARROLL

LEWIS CARROLL WAS the pseudonym of Charles Lutwidge Dodgson, a Rugby-educated lecturer in Mathematics at Oxford and the inventor of many educational board games. His books *Alice's Adventures in Wonderland* (1865) and *Through the Looking Glass* (1871) were inspired by a boat trip he took with the three young Liddell girls, Lorina, Alice and Edith, who were the daughters of the dean of his college. On publication the books were immediately condemned 'for not teaching anything nor containing any moral', a judgement which seems to have led to their instant success.

On going away to boarding school aged eight I was given two battered books: *Tom Brown's Schooldays* by Thomas Hughes and *Alice's Adventures in Wonderland*. Both scared the living daylights out of me. I did, however, think Tenniel's illustrations of Alice were quite lovely and I later managed to pluck up the courage to tackle *Through the Looking Glass* in the hope of seeing her again. I found it equally terrifying but well worth it for the Jabberwock.

> 'Twas brillig, and the slithy toves
> Did gyre and gimble in the wabe:
> All mimsy were the borogoves,
> And the mome raths outgrabe.
>
> 'Beware the Jabberwock, my son!
> The jaws that bite, the claws that catch!
> Beware the Jubjub bird, and shun
> The frumious Bandersnatch!'
>
> He took his vorpal sword in hand:
> Long time the manxome foe he sought —
> So rested he by the Tumtum tree,
> And stood awhile in thought.

And, as in uffish thought he stood,
   The Jabberwock, with eyes of flame,
Came whiffling through the tulgey wood,
   And burbled as it came!

One, two! One, two! And through and through
   The vorpal blade went snicker-snack!
He left it dead, and with its head
   He went galumphing back.

'And hast thou slain the Jabberwock?
   Come to my arms, my beamish boy!
O frabjous day! Callooh! Callay!'
   He chortled in his joy.

'Twas brillig, and the slithy toves
   Did gyre and gimble in the wabe:
All mimsy were the borogoves,
   And the mome raths outgrabe.

From The Hound of Heaven
⟹ 1913 ⟸

FRANCIS THOMPSON

FRANCIS THOMPSON HAD a tragic life. He was born in 1859 and educated at Ushaw College. He failed to pass his medical exams in Manchester and then failed to find an alternative career or even a living. He moved to London in 1885, became an opium addict and then a tramp, sustained only by his Catholic faith. He died of consumption in 1907.

Despite the awful life of the poet (of which I was blissfully unaware until compiling this book), I cannot help but associate this poem with home and happiness, as my mother would recite it at the slightest provocation – the words 'night', 'day', 'year', 'arches' and 'fled' being particular triggers.

I fled Him, down the nights and down the days;
I fled Him, down the arches of the years;
I fled Him, down the labyrinthine ways
    Of my own mind; and in the midst of tears
I hid from Him, and under running laughter.
                Up vistaed hopes I
sped;
                And shot,
precipitated,
Adown Titanic glooms of chasmèd fears,
From those strong Feet that followed, followed after
                But with unhurrying
chase,
                And unperturbèd pace,

    Deliberate speed, majestic instancy

They beat — and a

Voice beat

More instant than the

Feet —

   'All things betray thee, who betrayest me.'

I pleaded,

outlaw-wise,

By many a hearted casement, curtained red,

   Trellised with inter-twining charities,

(For though I knew His love who followèd,

               Yet was I sore

adread,

Lest, having Him, I should have naught beside);

But if one little casement parted wide,

   The gust of His approach would clash it to.

Fear wist not to evade as Love wist to pursue.

Across the margent of the world I fled,

   And troubled the gold gateways of the stars,

     Smiting for shelter on their clangèd bars,

           Fretted to dulcet

jars

And silvern chatter the pale ports o' the moon.

I said to Dawn: Be sudden — to Eve: Be soon,

   With thy young skyey blossoms heap me over

           From this tremendous

Lover!

Float thy vague veil about me lest He see!

   I tempted all His servitors but to find

My own betrayal in their constancy,

In faith to Him their fickleness to me,

   Their traitorous trueness and their loyal deceit.

To all swift things for swiftness did I sue,
   Clung to the whistling mane of every wind,
     But whether they swept, smoothly fleet,
  The long savannahs of the blue,
         Or whether,
Thunder-driven,
  They clanged His chariot 'thwart a heaven,
Plashy with flying lightnings round the spurn o' their feet —
  Fear wist not to evade as Love wist to pursue.
        Still with unhurrying
chase
        And unperturbèd pace
  Deliberate speed, majestic instancy,
        Came on the following
Feet,
        And a Voice above
their beat —
  'Naught shelters thee, who wilt not shelter Me.'

The Thought-Fox

———— 1975 ————

TED HUGHES

IT IS STRANGE how noise seems to help the creative process. In putting together this book I came across seven poets who mentioned sounds as a trigger for verse. These included the ticking of clocks, as here, rain on the roof or window, wind, a fire in the grate and the snoring of a dog.

> I imagine this midnight moment's forest:
> Something else is alive
> Beside the clock's loneliness
> And this blank page where my fingers move.
>
> Through the window I see no star:
> Something more near
> Though deeper within darkness
> Is entering the loneliness:
>
> Cold, delicately as the dark snow,
> A fox's nose touches twig, leaf;
> Two eyes serve a movement, that now
> And again now, and now, and now
>
> Sets neat prints into the snow
> Between trees, and warily a lame
> Shadow lags by stump and in hollow
> Of a body that is bold to come
>
> Across clearings, an eye,
> A widening deepening greenness,
> Brilliantly, concentratedly,
> Coming about its own business

Till, with a sudden sharp hot stink of fox
It enters the dark hole of the head.
The window is starless still; the clock ticks,
The page is printed.

8

DEFIANCE

THE ENGLISH HAVE such a magnificent history of defiance and dissent that this chapter might easily have been two or three times the length. Among the many things defied here are: complacency, age, illness, the Establishment, despair and, of course, the French. All the poems are soul-stirring and written with total conviction. I defy anyone to read or hear them without being moved.

Invictus

➤ 1875 ➤

W. E. HENLEY

THE SON OF a Gloucester bookseller, W. E. Henley suffered from tubercular arthritis from early childhood, through which he lost a foot. In 1873, aged 24, he spent a year in hospital in Edinburgh. The writing of 'Invictus', which means 'unconquerable', was part of the process of what he called 'seeing off my illness'. It seems to have worked, as he died in 1903, aged 54.

He met Robert Louis Stevenson in hospital and they collaborated on a number of plays. Stevenson claimed that Henley was the model for his *Treasure Island* character Long John Silver and described him as 'boisterous and piratic'.

> Out of the night that covers me,
>   Black as the Pit from pole to pole,
> I thank whatever gods may be
>   For my unconquerable soul.
> In the fell clutch of circumstance
>   I have not winced nor cried aloud.
> Under the bludgeonings of chance
>   My head is bloody, but unbowed.
> Beyond this place of wrath and tears
>   Looms but the Horror of the shade,
> And yet the menace of the years
>   Finds, and shall find, me unafraid.
> It matters not how strait the gate,
>   How charged with punishments the scroll,
> I am the master of my fate:
>   I am the captain of my soul.

'Who would true valour see' from The Pilgrim's Progress

———— 1684 ————

John Bunyan

JOHN BUNYAN WAS born near Bedford in 1628, the son of a tinsmith. He enlisted in the Parliamentary Army during the Civil War to spite his father for remarrying on the death of his mother. He believed himself responsible for the death of a fellow soldier who was shot while covering for him when he went absent without leave in 1645.

A true non-conformist Protestant, Bunyan was always highly suspicious of clergymen and ritual. He believed that the Word of God, as set down in the Bible, was all anyone needed to achieve salvation. Between 1661 and 1672 he was imprisoned for his refusal to deny 'his intention to preach' and during this time he wrote nine books. In 1675 he was re-imprisoned and started to write his best known work, *The Pilgrim's Progress*.

I read *The Pilgrim's Progress* on the train and, to my shame, found it rather hard-going. I'm not sure what I was expecting – a cross between the King James Bible and *The Lord of the Rings* perhaps – but no doubt the fault lies with me rather than the book.

> Who would true valour see,
> Let him come hither;
> One here will constant be,
> Come wind, come weather.
> There's no discouragement
> Shall make him once relent
> His first avowed intent
> To be a pilgrim.

Whoso beset him round
With dismal stories
Do but themselves confound;
His strength the more is.
No lion can him fright,
He'll with a giant fight,
But he will have a right
To be a pilgrim.

Hobgoblin, nor foul fiend
Can daunt his spirit:
He knows, he at the end
Shall life inherit.
Then fancies fly away,
He'll fear not what men say,
He'll labour night and day
To be a pilgrim.

'Do not go gentle into that good night'

—— 1952 ——

DYLAN THOMAS

DYLAN THOMAS was born in 1914 in Swansea and was educated at the city's grammar school, where his father was an English teacher. He did not speak Welsh. He worked as a journalist on a local newspaper for a while before moving to London in 1934.

His first volume of poetry was published in that same year. He married in 1937 and returned permanently to South Wales with his wife in 1949.

In 1950 Thomas embarked on a series of poetry-reading tours in the USA; he died in New York in 1953, from 'an insult to the brain', an American euphemism for alcoholic poisoning.

> Do not go gentle into that good night,
> Old age should burn and rave at close of day;
> Rage, rage against the dying of the light.
>
> Though wise men at their end know dark is right,
> Because their words had forked no lightning they
> Do not go gentle into that good night.
>
> Good men, the last wave by, crying how bright
> Their frail deeds might have danced in a green bay,
> Rage, rage against the dying of the light.
>
> Wild men who caught and sang the sun in flight,
> And learn, too late, they grieved it on its way,
> Do not go gentle into that good night.
>
> Grave men, near death, who see with blinding sight
> Blind eyes could blaze like meteors and be gay,
> Rage, rage against the dying of the light.

And you, my father, there on the sad height,
Curse, bless, me now with your fierce tears, I pray.
Do not go gentle into that good night.
Rage, rage against the dying of the light.

Jerusalem
——— 1804 ———

Words: WILLIAM BLAKE
Music: SIR HUBERT PARRY

WILLIAM BLAKE BELIEVED that Joseph of Arimathea, who gave up his tomb for the crucified Jesus Christ, had previously visited England with the child Jesus while trading tin. So Blake's answer to the questions of the first verse is yes.

Imprisoned for 12 years after the death of Christ, Joseph is reputed to have been kept alive by the Holy Grail (the cup that Jesus drank from during the Last Supper) until Emperor Vespasian ordered his release in AD 63. Joseph is then alleged to have taken the Grail, together with the Spear with which Jesus had been wounded on the cross, to England, where he founded the abbey at Glastonbury.

The music was written by Sir Hubert Parry, a musical historian and Director of the Royal College of Music, who was knighted in 1898.

The song 'Jerusalem' has been adopted by hundreds of British institutions, including regiments, schools, political parties and even the Women's Institute.

> And did those feet in ancient time
> Walk upon England's mountains green?
> And was the holy Lamb of God
> On England's pleasant pastures seen?
>
> And did the Countenance Divine
> Shine forth upon our clouded hills?
> And was Jerusalem builded here
> Among these dark Satanic Mills?

Bring me my Bow of burning gold!
Bring me my Arrows of desire!
Bring me my Spear! O clouds, unfold!
Bring me my Chariot of fire!

I will not cease from Mental Fight,
Nor shall my Sword sleep in my hand,
Till we have built Jerusalem
In England's green and pleasant land.

The English War
—— 1939 ——
DOROTHY L. SAYERS

DOROTHY L. SAYERS was born in the Fens in 1893, the daughter of a vicar. She married a journalist and was a hugely influential copywriter for an advertising agency. She created the fictional detective Lord Peter Wimsey and died in 1957.

> Praise God, now, for an English war —
> The grey tide and the sullen coast,
> The menace of the urgent hour,
> The single island, like a tower,
> Ringed with an angry host.
>
> This is the war that England knows,
> When all the world holds but one man —
> King Philip of the galleons,
> Louis, whose light outshone the sun's,
> The conquering Corsican.
>
> When Europe, like a prison door,
> Clangs; and the swift, enfranchised sea
> Runs narrower than a village brook;
> And men who love us not, yet look
> To us for liberty;
>
> When no allies are left, no help
> To count upon from alien hands,
> No waverers remain to woo,
> No more advice to listen to,
> And only England stands.

This is the war we always knew,
When every country keeps her own,
When Kent stands sentry in the lane
And Fenland guards her dyke and drain,
Cornwall, her cliffs of stone;

When from the Cinque Ports and the Wight,
From Plymouth Sound and Bristol Town,
There comes a noise that breaks our sleep,
Of the deep calling to the deep
Where the ships go up and down,

And near and far across the world
Hold open wide the water-gates,
And all the tall adventurers come
Homeward to England, and Drake's drum
Is beaten through the Straits.

This is the war that we have known
And fought in every hundred years,
Our sword, upon the last, steep path,
Forged by the hammer of our wrath
On the anvil of our fears.

Send us, O God, the will and power
To do as we have done before;
The men that ride the sea and air
Are the same men their fathers were
To fight the English war.

And send, O God, an English peace —
Some sense, some decency, perhaps
Some justice, too, if we are able,
With no sly jackals round our table,
Cringing for blood-stained scraps;

No dangerous dreams of wishful men
Whose homes are safe, who never feel
The flying death that swoops and stuns,
The kisses of the curtseying guns
Slavering their streets with steel;

No dreams, Lord God, but vigilance,
That we may keep, by might and main,
Inviolate seas, inviolate skies; —
But, if another tyrant rise,
Then we shall fight again

Ulysses

> 1842 <

ALFRED, LORD TENNYSON

BEFORE HIS MARRIAGE Tennyson had a special relationship, almost an infatuation, with Arthur Hallam, his fellow under-graduate at Trinity College, Cambridge, who died in 1833. Tennyson wrote this poem soon after Hallam's death, racked by grief but conscious 'that still life must be fought out to the end'.

Ulysses or Odysseus ('the hater'), was the Greek King of Ithaca who dreamt up the idea of the wooden horse during the siege of Troy. He is the hero of Homer's *Odyssey*. Here Tennyson presents him at the end of his reign, safely back home, but restless once more 'to drink life to the lees'.

It little profits that an idle King,
By this still hearth, among these barren crags,
Matched with an agèd wife, I mete and dole
Unequal laws unto a savage race,
That hoard, and sleep, and feed, and know not me.

I cannot rest from travel: I will drink
Life to the lees: all times I have enjoyed
Greatly, have suffer'd greatly, both with those
That loved me, and alone; on shore, and when
Through scudding drifts the rainy Hyades
Vext the dim sea: I am become a name;
For always roaming with a hungry heart
Much have I seen and known; cities of men
And manners, climates, councils, governments,
Myself not least, but honoured of them all;
And drunk delight of battle with my peers,
Far on the ringing plains of windy Troy.

I am a part of all that I have met;
Yet all experience is an arch wherethrough
Gleams that untravelled world, whose margin fades
For ever and for ever when I move.
How dull it is to pause, to make an end,
To rust unburnished, not to shine in use!
As though to breathe were life. Life piled on life
Were all too little, and of one to me
Little remains: but every hour is saved
From that eternal silence, something more,
A bringer of new things; and vile it were
For some three suns to store and hoard myself,
And this gray spirit yearning in desire
To follow knowledge like a sinking star,
Beyond the utmost bound of human thought.

This is my son, mine own Telemachus,
To whom I leave the sceptre and the isle —
Well-loved of me, discerning to fulfil
This labour, by slow prudence to make mild
A rugged people, and through soft degrees
Subdue them to the useful and the good.
Most blameless is he, centred in the sphere
Of common duties, decent not to fail
In offices of tenderness, and pay
Meet adoration to my household gods,
When I am gone. He works his work, I mine.

There lies the port; the vessel puffs her sail:
There gloom the dark broad seas. My mariners,
Souls that have toiled, and wrought, and thought with me —
That ever with a frolic welcome took
The thunder and the sunshine, and opposed
Free hearts, free foreheads — you and I are old;

Old age hath yet his honour and his toil;
Death closes all: but something ere the end,
Some work of noble note, may yet be done,
Not unbecoming men that strove with Gods.
The lights begin to twinkle from the rocks:
The long day wanes: the slow moon climbs: the deep
Moans round with many voices. Come, my friends,
'Tis not too late to seek a newer world.
Push off, and sitting well in order smite
The sounding furrows; for my purpose holds
To sail beyond the sunset, and the baths
Of all the western stars, until I die.
It may be that the gulfs will wash us down:
It may be we shall touch the Happy Isles,
And see the great Achilles, whom we knew.
Though much is taken, much abides; and though
We are not now that strength which in old days
Moved earth and heaven, that which we are, we are;
One equal temper of heroic hearts,
Made weak by time and fate, but strong in will
To strive, to seek, to find, and not to yield.

'This day is call'd the feast of Crispian' from Henry V, Act IV, Scene III

————— 1599 —————

WILLIAM SHAKESPEARE

THE COBBLER CRISPIN is the patron saint of shoemakers (crepis is the Greek word for 'shoe',) one of two Roman brothers, Crispin and Crispian, who went to France in AD 303 to spread Christianity. Crispin was martyred on 25 October 303 and it was on this day, in 1415, that Henry V led his men into battle against the French at Agincourt, where the longbow played such a crucial part in the English victory.

This is the speech that Henry V makes to his men before going into battle. Shakespeare treats the two brothers, Crispin and Crispian, as one and the same.

> This day is call'd the feast of Crispian:
> He that outlives this day, and comes safe home,
> Will stand a-tiptoe when this day is nam'd,
> And rouse him at the name of Crispian.
> He that shall live this day, and see old age,
> Will yearly on the vigil feast his neighbours,
> And say, 'To-morrow is Saint Crispian':
> Then will he strip his sleeve and show his scars,
> And say, 'These wounds I had on Crispin's day.'
> Old men forget: yet all shall be forgot,
> But he'll remember with advantages
> What feats he did that day. Then shall our names,
> Familiar in his mouth as household words,
> Harry the King, Bedford and Exeter,
> Warwick and Talbot, Salisbury and Gloucester,
> Be in their flowing cups freshly remember'd.
> This story shall the good man teach his son;

And Crispin Crispian shall ne'er go by,
From this day to the ending of the world,
But we in it shall be rememberèd;
We few, we happy few, we band of brothers;
For he to-day that sheds his blood with me
Shall be my brother; be he ne'er so vile,
This day shall gentle his condition:
And gentlemen in England, now a-bed
Shall think themselves accurs'd they were not here,
And hold their manhoods cheap whiles any speaks
That fought with us upon Saint Crispin's day.

'As I lay asleep in Italy' from
The Mask of Anarchy
⟹ 1819 ⟸

PERCY BYSSHE SHELLEY

SHELLEY WAS INSPIRED to write *The Mask of Anarchy* after reading about the Peterloo massacre. On 16 August 1819 a crowd assembled in St Peter's Field in Manchester for a political rally on the issue of parliamentary reform. The mounted yeomanry tried to arrest one of the speakers, Orator Hunt, and in the ensuing melee 11 people, including two women, were killed and more than 500 were injured.

Written while in self-imposed exile in Italy, Shelley's poem quickly became a revolutionary hymn.

[...]

As I lay asleep in Italy
There came a voice from over the Sea,
And with great power it forth led me
To walk in the visions of Poesy.

I met Murder on the way —
He had a mask like Castlereagh —
Very smooth he looked, yet grim;
Seven blood-hounds followed him:

All were fat; and well they might
Be in admirable plight,
For one by one, and two by two,
He tossed the human hearts to chew
Which from his wide cloak he drew.

Next came Fraud, and he had on,
Like Eldon, an ermined gown;
His big tears, for he wept well,
Turned to mill-stones as they fell.

And the little children, who
Round his feet played to and fro,
Thinking every tear a gem,
Had their brains knocked out by them.

Clothed with the Bible, as with light,
And the shadows of the night,
Like Sidmouth, next, Hypocrisy
On a crocodile rode by.

And many more Destructions played
In this ghastly masquerade,
All disguised, even to the eyes,
Like Bishops, lawyers, peers, or spies.

Last came Anarchy: he rode
On a white horse, splashed with blood;
He was pale even to the lips,
Like Death in the Apocalypse.

And he wore a kingly crown;
And in his grasp a sceptre shone;
On his brow this mark I saw —
'I AM GOD, AND KING, AND LAW!'

[...]

'And these words shall then become
Like Oppression's thundered doom
Ringing through each heart and brain,
Heard again — again — again —

'Rise like Lions after slumber
In unvanquishable number —
Shake your chains to earth like dew
Which in sleep had fallen on you —
Ye are many — they are few.'

Into Battle

— 1915 —

JULIAN GRENFELL

EDUCATED AT ETON and Oxford, Julian Grenfell joined the regular army in 1910 and was sent to France in 1914. He won the DSO and was killed in action at Ypres in May 1915, aged 27. This poem was published in *The Times* after his death.

The naked earth is warm with Spring,
    And with green grass and bursting trees
Leans to the sun's gaze glorying,
    And quivers in the sunny breeze;

And life is colour and warmth and light,
    And a striving evermore for these;
And he is dead who will not fight;
    And who dies fighting has increase.

The fighting man shall from the sun
    Take warmth, and life from the glowing earth;
Speed with the light-foot winds to run,
    And with the trees to newer birth;
And find, when fighting shall be done,
    Great rest, and fullness after dearth.

All the bright company of Heaven
    Hold him in their high comradeship,
The Dog-Star, and the Sisters Seven,
    Orion's Belt and sworded hip.

The woodland trees that stand together,
    They stand to him each one a friend;
They gently speak in the windy weather;
    They guide to valley and ridge's end.

The kestrel hovering by day,
  And the little owls that call by night,
Bid him be swift and keen as they,
  As keen of ear, as swift of sight.

The blackbird sings to him, 'Brother, brother,
  If this be the last song you shall sing,
Sing well, for you may not sing another;
  Brother, sing.'

In dreary, doubtful, waiting hours,
  Before the brazen frenzy starts,
The horses show him nobler powers;
  O patient eyes, courageous hearts!

And when the burning moment breaks,
  And all things else are out of mind,
And only joy of battle takes
  Him by the throat, and makes him blind,

Through joy and blindness he shall know,
  Not caring much to know, that still
Nor lead nor steel shall reach him, so
  That it be not the Destined Will.

The thundering line of battle stands,
  And in the air Death moans and sings:
But Day shall clasp him with strong hands,
  And Night shall fold him in soft wings.

'What though the field be lost?'
from Paradise Lost
1667

JOHN MILTON

IN 1644, FIVE years before the execution of Charles I, Milton wrote, 'Give me the liberty to know, to utter, and to argue freely according to my conscience above all liberties.'

In this extract (much admired by Winston Churchill) Milton gives Satan his say.

> What though the field be lost?
> All is not lost; the unconquerable Will,
> And study of revenge, immortal hate,
> And courage never to submit or yield:
> And what is else not to be overcome?
> That glory never shall his wrath or might
> Extort from me. To bow and sue for grace
> With suppliant knee, and deify his power
> Who, from the terror of this arm, so late
> Doubted his Empire, that were low indeed;
> That were an ignominy and shame beneath
> This downfall; since by fate the strength of Gods,
> And this empyreal substance, cannot fail;
> Since, through experience of this great event,
> In arms not worse, in foresight much advanced,
> We may with more successful hope resolve
> To wage by force or guile eternal war,
> Irreconcilable to our grand foe,
> Who now triumphs, and in th' excess of joy
> Sole reigning holds the tyranny of Heaven.

'Say not the struggle nought availeth'
1855
Arthur Hugh Clough

Arthur Hugh Clough was born 1819 and educated at Rugby. He went on to Oxford, where he was mortified to achieve only a second-class degree. In due course, however, he became the Principal of University Hall, London, and was an examiner in the Education Office. He died in Florence in 1861.

Winston Churchill quoted this poem when he was in Canada in 1941 rallying the Empire to the defence of freedom.

Say not the struggle nought availeth,
    The labour and the wounds are vain,
The enemy faints not, nor faileth,
    And as things have been, things remain.

If hopes were dupes, fears may be liars;
    It may be, in yon smoke concealed,
Your comrades chase e'en now the fliers,
    And, but for you, possess the field.

For while the tired waves, vainly breaking,
    Seem here no painful inch to gain,
Far back, through creeks and inlets making,
    Comes, silent, flooding in, the main.

And not by eastern windows only,
    When daylight comes, comes in the light;
In front the sun climbs slow, how slowly,
    But westward, look, the land is bright!

9

KINGSHIP

M Y FATHER HAS a theory that older sons are likely to be conservative, perhaps because they are happier with the status quo. Certainly I am. At a recent business drinks party in London we somehow got onto the subject of patriotism and the Queen. At some point or other, without really thinking anything of it, I must have said that I loved her. I very soon found myself at the centre of an increasingly heated full-blown row, with wild-eyed rationalists demanding to know how I could possibly defend the hereditary principle, etc., etc., and actually love someone I had never even met.

Well, the fact of the matter is that I can and do, just as the vast majority of us can and do love the Queen; and when Prince Charles becomes King, despite the media's constant insistence to the contrary, we will love him in his turn.

Preparations
C. 1610
ANONYMOUS

THIS POEM IS presumed to have been written during the reign of either James I or Charles I, when it was still considered 'a duteous thing to show all honour to an earthly King'.

Yet if His Majesty, our sovereign lord,
Should of his own accord
Friendly himself invite,
And say 'I'll be your guest to-morrow night,'
How should we stir ourselves, call and command
All hands to work! 'Let no man idle stand!

'Set me fine Spanish tables in the hall;
See they be fitted all;
Let there be room to eat
And order taken that there want no meat.
See every sconce and candlestick made bright,
That without tapers they may give a light.

'Look to the presence: are the carpets spread,
The dazie o'er the head,
The cushions in the chairs,
And all the candles lighted on the stairs?
Perfume the chambers, and in any case
Let each man give attendance to his place!'

Thus, if a King were coming, would we do;
And 'twere good reason too;
For 'tis a duteous thing
To show all honour to an earthly King,
And after all our travail and our cost,
So he be pleased, to think no labour lost.

But at the coming of the King of Heaven
All's set at six and seven;
We wallow in our sin,
Christ cannot find a chamber in the inn.
We entertain Him always like a stranger,
And, as at first, still lodge Him in the manger.

"'Twas God the word that spake it'
===== 1553 =====
QUEEN ELIZABETH I

QUEEN ELIZABETH I was arguably our greatest monarch, inheriting a throne torn between religious extremes. She refrained from persecuting Catholics, however, while embracing Protestantism as a patriotic necessity, subsequently presiding over a national rebirth.

This verse, which she composed before she was Queen to answer inquisitors questioning her views on the presence of Christ in the sacrament (questions to which the wrong answer could lead to the Tower), is typical of the woman who vowed when she became Queen herself 'not to open windows into men's souls'.

'Twas God the word that spake it,
He took the bread and brake it;
And what the word did make it;
That I believe, and take it.

The Old Squire
1910

WILFRID SCAWEN BLUNT

WILFRID SCAWEN BLUNT was born in 1840. He joined the diplomatic service and he travelled widely with his wife after he married. In 1872 he inherited Crabbet Park in Sussex, where he bred horses. During the course of a series of visits to India he became an ardent critic of Empire. He opposed the occupation of Egypt, for example, and championed the cause of Ireland. He died in 1922.

Perhaps his extensive travels helped Blunt to express the idea of an Englishman's home as his castle so simply. His writing resounds with a sense of belonging and a love of the English countryside.

> I like the hunting of the hare
>   Better than that of the fox;
> I like the joyous morning air,
>   And the crowing of the cocks.
>
> I like the calm of the early fields,
>   The ducks asleep by the lake,
> The quiet hour which Nature yields,
>   Before mankind is awake.
>
> I like the pheasants and feeding things
>   Of the unsuspicious morn;
> I like the flap of the wood-pigeon's wings
>   As she rises from the corn.
>
> I like the blackbird's shriek, and his rush
>   From the turnips as I pass by,
> And the partridge hiding her head in a bush
>   For her young ones cannot fly.

I like these things, and I like to ride
   When all the world is in bed,
To the top of the hill where the sky grows wide,
   And where the sun grows red.

The beagles at my horse heels trot
   In silence after me;
There's Ruby, Roger, Diamond, Dot,
   Old Slut and Margery, —

A score of names well used, and dear,
   The names my childhood knew;
The horn, with which I rouse their cheer,
   Is the horn my father blew.

I like the hunting of the hare
   Better than that of the fox;
The new world still is all less fair
   Than the old world it mocks.

I covet not a wider range
   Than these dear manors give;
I take my pleasures without change,
   And as I lived I live.

I leave my neighbours to their thought;
   My choice it is, and pride,
On my own lands to find my sport,
   In my own fields to ride.

The hare herself no better loves
   The field where she was bred,
Than I the habit of these groves,
   My own inherited.

I know my quarries every one,
    The meuse where she sits low;
The road she chose to-day was run
    A hundred years ago.

The lags, the gills, the forest ways,
    The hedgerows one and all,
These are the kingdoms of my chase,
    And bounded by my wall;

Nor has the world a better thing,
    Though one should search it round,
Than thus to live one's own sole King,
    Upon one's own sole ground.

I like the hunting of the hare;
    It brings me, day to day,
The memory of old days as fair,
    With dead men passed away.

To these, as homeward still I ply
    And pass the churchyard gate,
Where all are laid as I must lie,
    I stop and raise my hat.

I like the hunting of the hare;
    New sports I hold in scorn.
I like to be as my fathers were,
    In the days e'er I was born.

God Save the King

=> 1745 <=

Words: HENRY CAREY (ATTRIBUTED)
Music: DR THOMAS ARNE

THE WORDS TO the 1745 version of the British national anthem have been attributed to several different authors but the most likely candidate is the comic dramatist Henry Carey. He also wrote the song 'Sally in our Alley' and coined the nickname 'Namby-Pamby' for the poet Ambrose Philips.

However, the first two verses were published more than a hundred years earlier and it was probably the appropriately named Dr John Bull who was responsible. He was the Organist at Hereford Cathedral and then Professor of Music at Gresham College from 1597 to 1607. The line 'God save the King' is taken from 1 Samuel, 10:24: 'And all the people shouted and said "God save the King".'

Dr Thomas Arne, who also composed the music for 'Rule, Britannia', specialised in setting drama to music, between 1733 and his death in 1778 working for theatres in Drury Lane, Covent Garden and Stratford-upon-Avon.

The longer version of the anthem became established during the 1745 Jacobite Rebellion, when it also included the following verse:

> Lord, grant that Marshal Wade,
> May by thy mighty aid,
> Victory bring.
> May he sedition hush and like a torrent rush,
> Rebellious Scots to crush,
> God save the King!

God save our gracious King,
Long live our noble King,
God save the King!
Send him victorious,
Happy and glorious,
Long to reign over us;
God save the King!

O Lord our God arise,
Scatter his enemies,
And make them fall;
Confound their politics,
Frustrate their knavish tricks,
On Thee our hopes we fix:
God save us all!

Thy choicest gifts in store
On him be pleased to pour;
Long may he reign;
May he defend our laws,
And ever give us cause
To sing with hearts and voice,
'God save the King!'

From ev'ry latent foe,
From the assassin's blow,
God save the King!
O'er him thine arm extend,
For Britain's sake defend,
Our father, prince and friend,
God save the King!

From An Horatian Ode upon Cromwell's Return from Ireland

————— 1650 —————

ANDREW MARVELL

BORN IN YORKSHIRE in 1621 and educated at Cambridge, Andrew Marvell then went travelling in Europe, perhaps to avoid the Civil War. He became tutor to the daughter of Lord Fairfax, the Lord General of the Parliamentary Forces, which makes this poem, with its sympathetic recognition of the integrity and dignity of King Charles I at his execution, all the more surprising.

In 1657 Marvell began work as an assistant to Milton (who was blind by this time) in the Secretaryship of Foreign Tongues to Cromwell's Council of State. He was MP for Hull from 1659 until his death in 1678 and helped to secure Milton's release from prison after the Restoration.

> He nothing common did or mean
> Upon that memorable scene;
> But with his keener eye
> The axe's edge did try:
>
> Nor called the Gods with vulgar spite
> To vindicate his helpless right,
> But bowed his comely head
> Down, as upon a bed.

The Vicar of Bray
17TH CENTURY

Words: ANONYMOUS
Music: ANONYMOUS

THOUGH REPEATEDLY ALTERED to suit the times, the words to this popular song were inspired by the notorious sixteenth-century Vicar of Bray in Berkshire, who managed to keep his living throughout the reigns of Henry VIII, Edward VI, Bloody Mary and Elizabeth I.

President Mitterrand, who was naturally a republican, is reputed to have cited this poem as evidence of the unthinking loyalty the English give to their monarchs. He was not being entirely fair. Though staunch royalists, if a King or Queen really does not suit, the English do have a record of replacing them with more congenial alternatives.

> In good King Charles's golden days,
> When loyalty no harm meant,
> A zealous high churchman was I,
> And so I gained preferment.
> To teach my flock I never miss'd,
> Kings are by God appointed,
> And damned are those who dare resist
> Or touch the Lord's anointed.
>
> *Chorus*
> And this is law that I'll maintain
> Until my dying day, Sir,
> That whatsoever King may reign,
> Still I'll be the Vicar of Bray, Sir!
>
> When Royal James possessed the crown
> And pop'ry came in fashion,
> The Penal Laws I hooted down

And read the Declaration,
The Church of Rome I found would fit,
Full well my constitution
And I had been a Jesuit,
But for the Revolution.

Chorus . . .

When William was our King declar'd
To ease the nation's grievance,
With this new wind about I steered
And swore to him allegiance;
Old principles I did revoke,
Set conscience at a distance,
Passive obedience was a joke,
A jest was non-resistance.

Chorus . . .

When Royal Anne became our Queen
Then Church of England's Glory
Another face of things was seen
And I became a Tory
Occasional conformists base
I blamed their moderation
And thought the Church in danger was
By such prevarication.

Chorus . . .

When George in pudding time came o'er
And moderate men looked big, Sir,
I turned a cat-in-the-pan once more,
And so became a Whig, Sir,
   And thus preferment I procured

From our new faith's defender.
And almost every day abjured
The Pope and the Pretender.

Chorus . . .

The illustrious house of Hanover
And Protestant succession,
To these I do allegiance swear, –
While they can keep possession;
For in my faith and loyalty,
I never more will falter,
And George my lawful King shall be
Until the times do alter.

Chorus . . .

A Charm

⇒ 1907 ⇐

RUDYARD KIPLING

WILLIAM PITT THE Elder, the Great Commoner, said in 1767, 'The poorest man may in his cottage bid defiance to all the forces of the Crown! The wind may enter, the rain may enter, but the King of England cannot enter!' It is surely one of the primary duties of the monarch to uphold our ancient freedoms so that each one of us may aspire, in our own sphere, to be 'a King indeed'.

Take of English earth as much
As either hand may rightly clutch.
In the taking of it breathe
Prayer for all who lie beneath.
Not the great nor well-bespoke,
But the mere uncounted folk
Of whose life and death is none
Report or lamentation.
  Lay that earth upon thy heart,
  And thy sickness shall depart!
It shall sweeten and make whole
Fevered breath and festered soul.
It shall mightily restrain
Over-busied hand and brain.
It shall ease thy mortal strife
'Gainst the immortal woe of life,
  Till thyself, restored, shall prove
  By what grace the Heavens do move.
Take of English flowers these —
Spring's full-faced primroses,
Summer's wild wide-hearted rose,
Autumn's wall-flower of the close,

And, thy darkness to illume,
Winter's bee-thronged ivy-bloom.
Seek and serve them where they bide
From Candlemas to Christmas-tide,
    For these simples, used aright,
    Can restore a failing sight.
These shall cleanse and purify
Webbed and inward-turning eye;
These shall show thee treasure hid,
Thy familiar fields amid;
And reveal (which is thy need)
Every man a King indeed!

'In times when nothing stood'
1977
PHILIP LARKIN

PHILIP LARKIN WROTE this poem on the Queen's Silver Jubilee, the 25th anniversary of her Coronation.

I once got talking to a man on the train who told me he was 92 and had been born during the First World War. He asked what I was reading and, when I showed him the cover of Larkin's *Collected Works*, he admitted to never having heard of him. I showed him 'The Mower' and several other poems and he volunteered that he, too, in 1970, had had a bit of a 'we're-all-going-to-hell-in-a-handcart' moment: children all yobbos, country going to the dogs, divorce made easy, etc., etc. But he also said that he gradually realised that things do stand, that people are always people and that although the Queen was one 'constant good' there were many others. 'Poor Mr Larkin,' he said, 'but I'm sure he got over it.'

> In times when nothing stood
> but worsened, or grew strange,
> there was one constant good:
> she did not change.

'This royal throne of Kings, this sceptr'd isle' from Richard II, Act II, Scene I

—— 1595 ——

WILLIAM SHAKESPEARE

SHAKESPEARE REFERS REPEATEDLY to the royal nature of England. This speech is so familiar it was remarkably easy to learn.

John of Gaunt, nearing death and filled with dread at the prospect of Civil War, delivers this glorious evocation of England. His son, arbitrarily exiled by the King, eventually deposes and replaces Richard II as Henry IV.

This royal throne of Kings, this sceptr'd isle,
This earth of majesty, this seat of Mars,
This other Eden, demi-paradise,
This fortress built by Nature for herself
Against infection and the hand of war,
This happy breed of men, this little world,
This precious stone set in the silver sea,
Which serves it in the office of a wall,
Or as a moat defensive to a house,
Against the envy of less happier lands,
This blessed plot, this earth, this realm, this England,
This nurse, this teeming womb of royal Kings,
Fear'd by their breed and famous by their birth,
Renowned for their deeds as far from home, —
For Christian service and true chivalry, —

The King's Breakfast
====> 1924 <====

A. A. Milne

THIS WAS ANOTHER of my mother's favourite poems, inevitably recited at breakfast.

A. A. Milne was born in 1882 and went to Westminster and Cambridge. He was assistant editor of *Punch* from 1906 to 1914 and spent the First World War as a signalling officer in the Royal Warwickshire Regiment. After the war, he worked on a series of stage comedies between 1919 and 1929 and produced a dramatisation of Kenneth Grahame's *The Wind in the Willows*. He is most famous for his verses and stories for children, including *Winnie-the-Pooh*, published in 1926, and *The House at Pooh Corner*, published in 1928. He died in 1956.

The King asked
The Queen, and
The Queen asked
The Dairymaid:
'Could we have some butter for
The Royal slice of bread?'
The Queen asked the Dairymaid,
The Dairymaid
Said, 'Certainly,
I'll go and tell the cow
Now
Before she goes to bed.'

The Dairymaid
She curtsied,
And went and told
The Alderney:
'Don't forget the butter for

[160]

The Royal slice of bread.'
The Alderney
Said sleepily:
'You'd better tell
His Majesty
That many people nowadays
Like marmalade
Instead.'

The Dairymaid
Said, 'Fancy!'
And went to
Her Majesty.
She curtsied to the Queen, and
She turned a little red:
'Excuse me,
Your Majesty,
For taking of
The liberty,
But marmalade is tasty, if
It's very
Thickly
Spread.'

The Queen said
'Oh!:
And went to
His Majesty:
'Talking of the butter for
The Royal slice of bread,
Many people
Think that
Marmalade
Is nicer.

Would you like to try a little
Marmalade
Instead?'

The King said,
'Bother!'
And then he said,
'Oh, deary me!'
The King sobbed, 'Oh, deary me!'
And went back to bed.
'Nobody,'
He whimpered,
'Could call me
A fussy man;
I only want
A little bit
Of butter for
My bread!'

The Queen said,
'There, there!'
And went to
The Dairymaid.
The Dairymaid
Said, 'There, there!'
And went to the shed.
The cow said,
'There, there!
I didn't really
Mean it;
Here's milk for his porringer,
And butter for his bread.'

The Queen took
The butter
And brought it to
His Majesty;
The King said,
'Butter, eh?'
And bounced out of bed.
'Nobody,' he said,
As he kissed her
Tenderly,
'Nobody,' he said,
As he slid down the banisters,
'Nobody,
My darling,
Could call me
A fussy man —
BUT
I do like a little bit of butter to my bread!'

10

LOSS

O N READING THROUGH these ten poems it occurs to me that by loss here I mean death. All of them seem to take for granted our intimate involvement with nature, with sunsets, rivers, hills, and to acknowledge that these things remain after an individual life has ended. Auden's poem is alone here in being devoid of a single note of hope, but even then he still exposes the depth of his feelings. And by calling upon such a diverse list of things to respond to his grief – the aeroplanes, doves, policemen, clocks, etc. – he simultaneously affirms the richness of life.

The Dead (Sonnet IV)
⟹ 1914 ⟸
RUPERT BROOKE

RUPERT BROOKE WAS born in Rugby in 1887, the son of a housemaster at the school, and went on to be a Scholar at King's College, Cambridge. W. B. Yeats described him as 'the handsomest man in England'. Before the First World War he had a nervous breakdown and visited Australia, Canada, New Zealand and the South Sea Islands. It is alleged that he fathered a daughter in Tahiti.

In 1914 he joined the Royal Naval Voluntary Reserve and died of blood poisoning on his way to the Dardanelles, aged 28.

These hearts were woven of human joys and cares,
    Washed marvellously with sorrow, swift to mirth.
The years had given them kindness. Dawn was theirs,
    And sunset, and the colours of the earth.
These had seen movement, and heard music; known
    Slumber and waking; loved; gone proudly friended;
Felt the quick stir of wonder; sat alone;
    Touched flowers and furs and cheeks. All this is ended.

There are waters blown by changing winds to laughter
And lit by the rich skies, all day. And after,
    Frost, with a gesture, stays the waves that dance
And wandering loveliness. He leaves a white
    Unbroken glory, a gathered radiance,
A width, a shining peace, under the night.

Requiem
1887
ROBERT LOUIS STEVENSON

BORN IN 1850, Robert Louis Stevenson went to Edinburgh University in 1867 to read engineering. He switched to law and became an advocate in 1875, although he never practised. He canoed around France and Belgium and travelled by emigrant ship to California in 1879.

The publication of his novel *Treasure Island* in 1883 and then *The Strange Case of Dr Jekyll and Mr Hyde* in 1886 made his name and he wrote many novels, short stories, poems, essays and books on travel. He always had a leaning towards morally ambiguous heroes. 'If your morals make you dreary,' he said, 'depend upon it, they are wrong.'

He settled in Samoa in 1888 and died suddenly there in 1894, having never taken his writing very seriously, once saying, 'Fiction is to grown men, what play is to a child.'

> Under the wide and starry sky,
> Dig the grave and let me lie.
> Glad did I live and gladly die,
> And I laid me down with a will.
>
> This be the verse you grave for me:
> Here he lies where he longed to be;
> Here is the sailor, home from the sea,
> And the hunter home from the hill.

'Nothing is here for tears . . .'
from Samson Agonistes
1671
JOHN MILTON

MILTON'S TRAGEDY ABOUT the end of Samson's life from the Book of Judges, when he is a prisoner of the Philistines and blind, is assumed to have been written after the restoration of Charles II, when the circumstances mirror Milton's own.

> Nothing is here for tears, nothing to wail
> Or knock the breast; no weakness, no contempt,
> Dispraise or blame; nothing but well and fair,
> And what may quiet us in a death so noble.

Epitaph
⟹ 1618 ⟸

SIR WALTER RALEIGH

SIR WALTER RALEIGH wrote this verse the night before his execution and it was found in his Bible at the Gate House in Westminster.

> Even such is Time, which takes in trust
> Our youth, our joys, and all we have,
> And pays us but with age and dust;
> Who in the dark and silent grave,
> When we have wandered all our ways,
> Shuts up the story of our days:
> And from which earth, and grave, and dust,
> The Lord will raise me up, I trust.

Song
1862
CHRISTINA ROSSETTI

CHRISTINA ROSSETTI, THE sister of the Pre-Raphaelite painter Dante Gabriel Rossetti, was born in London in 1830. She lived at home looking after her mother and working for her church. She was briefly engaged to the painter James Collinson but broke it off when he became a Catholic in 1850. From then on she began to write articles which were published in the Pre-Raphaelite magazine *The Germ*. She died in 1894, having been an invalid for many years.

When I am dead, my dearest,
　　Sing no sad songs for me;
Plant thou no roses at my head,
　　Nor shady cypress tree:
Be the green grass above me
　　With showers and dewdrops wet:
And if thou wilt, remember,
　　And if thou wilt, forget.

I shall not see the shadows,
　　I shall not feel the rain;
I shall not hear the nightingale
　　Sing on as if in pain;
And dreaming through the twilight
　　That doth not rise nor set,
Haply I may remember,
　　And haply may forget.

Remember

⟹ 1862 ⟸

CHRISTINA ROSSETTI

Remember me when I am gone away,
   Gone far away into the silent land;
   When you can no more hold me by the hand,
Nor I half turn to go yet turning stay.
Remember me when no more day by day
   You tell me of our future that you planned:
   Only remember me; you understand
It will be late to counsel then or pray.
Yet if you should forget me for a while
   And afterwards remember, do not grieve:
   For if the darkness and corruption leave
   A vestige of the thoughts that once I had,
Better by far you should forget and smile
   Than that you should remember and be sad.

Crossing the Bar
⟹ 1889 ⟸

ALFRED, LORD TENNYSON

TENNYSON WROTE THIS poem when he was 80, and it was apparently read at the funeral of an old naval friend of his, a contemporary from childhood, who drowned while out sailing off the Isle of Wight.

> Sunset and evening star,
>   And one clear call for me!
> And may there be no moaning of the bar,
>   When I put out to sea,
>
> But such a tide as moving seems asleep,
>   Too full for sound and foam,
> When that which drew from out the boundless deep
>   Turns again home.
>
> Twilight and evening bell,
>   And after that the dark!
> And may there be no sadness of farewell,
>   When I embark;
>
> For tho' from out our bourne of Time and Place
>   The flood may bear me far,
> I hope to see my Pilot face to face
>   When I have crost the bar.

Funeral Blues
1936

W. H. AUDEN

LIKE MANY OTHER people, I first came across this poem when I saw the film *Four Weddings and a Funeral*, and the simplicity of Auden's poetry seems to work especially well in the context of that scene. Despite the Marxism with which he responded to the chaos and anarchy of the inter-war years, Auden re-found his faith in the individual and in Christianity in the 1940s.

Stop all the clocks, cut off the telephone,
Prevent the dog from barking with a juicy bone,
Silence the pianos and with muffled drum
Bring out the coffin, let the mourners come.

Let aeroplanes circle moaning overhead
Scribbling on the sky the message He Is Dead,
Put crêpe bows round the white necks of the public doves,
Let the traffic policemen wear black cotton gloves.

He was my North, my South, my East and West,
My working week and my Sunday rest,
My noon, my midnight, my talk, my song;
I thought that love would last for ever: I was wrong.

The stars are not wanted now: put out every one;
Pack up the moon and dismantle the sun;
Pour away the ocean and sweep up the wood.
For nothing now can ever come to any good.

The Trees

— 1967 —

PHILIP LARKIN

THIS POEM WAS read at my grandmother-in-law's funeral – she
devoutly believed that death was a new beginning.

> The trees are coming into leaf
> Like something almost being said;
> The recent buds relax and spread,
> Their greenness is a kind of grief.
>
> Is it that they are born again
> And we grow old? No, they die too.
> Their yearly trick of looking new
> Is written down in rings of grain.
>
> Yet still the unresting castles thresh
> In fullgrown thickness every May.
> Last year is dead, they seem to say,
> Begin afresh, afresh, afresh.

Holy Sonnet (III)
1609

JOHN DONNE

I HAD ALWAYS ASSUMED that Donne wrote this sonnet towards the end of his life, when he was a well-established and hugely successful Anglican priest. In fact, he was 37 when he wrote it, during the 14 years of disgrace, his secret marriage to the daughter of a rich and influential Surrey land-owner against her father's wishes, leaving him unable to find a job.

Death, be not proud, though some have callèd thee
    Mighty and dreadful, for thou art not so;
    For those whom thou think'st thou dost overthrow
Die not, poor Death, nor yet canst thou kill me.
From rest and sleep, which but thy pictures be,
    Much pleasure — then, from thee much more must flow;
    And soonest our best men with thee do go,
Rest of their bones and soul's delivery.
Thou'rt slave to fate, chance, Kings, and desperate men,
    And dost with poison, war, and sickness dwell;
    And poppy or charms can make us sleep as well,
And better than thy stroke. Why swell'st thou then?
    One short sleep past, we wake eternally,
    And Death shall be no more. Death, thou shalt die.

11

HOME

A<small>FTER A RECENT</small> parent teacher meeting at my younger sons' school a gang of us parents went on to the pub for supper. Someone asked what we wanted for our children and after several hours of very earnest discussion we came to the rather obvious conclusion that we wanted them to be happy and, if possible, to like us.

For me home is intimately linked to childhood and children, a place of security and nurturing and love. In an article in the *Daily Telegraph* in the Spring of 2007, arguing for a new English Bill of Rights, the socialist singer Billy Bragg dismissed 'an Englishman's home is his castle' as not much of a national rallying cry. I disagree. England is a country where we can expect to create the home of our choice without the interference of tyrants or busybodies: a castle of our hopes and love. I do think that is something worth shouting about – and defending.

If

1910

RUDYARD KIPLING

LOVE OF COUNTRY, love of family and love of home are all
intimately bound up with a sense of belonging – belonging
to the past, the present and the future. A nation and a family are
both communities of the dead, the living and those as yet unborn.

In this poem Rudyard Kipling ponders the obstacles and setbacks
his son might encounter and the ways in which he should face
them.

If you can keep your head when all about you
    Are losing theirs and blaming it on you;
If you can trust yourself when all men doubt you,
    But make allowance for their doubting too;
If you can wait and not be tired by waiting,
    Or, being lied about, don't deal in lies,
Or being hated, don't give way to hating,
    And yet don't look too good, nor talk too wise;

If you can dream — and not make dreams your master;
    If you can think — and not make thoughts your aim;
If you can meet with Triumph and Disaster
    And treat those two impostors just the same;
If you can bear to hear the truth you've spoken
    Twisted by knaves to make a trap for fools,
Or watch the things you gave your life to, broken,
    And stoop and build 'em up with worn-out tools;

If you can make one heap of all your winnings
　　And risk it on one turn of pitch-and-toss,
And lose, and start again at your beginnings
　　And never breathe a word about your loss;
If you can force your heart and nerve and sinew
　　To serve your turn long after they are gone,
And so hold on when there is nothing in you
　　Except the Will which says to them: 'Hold on!'

If you can talk with crowds and keep your virtue,
　　Or walk with Kings — nor lose the common touch;
If neither foes nor loving friends can hurt you,
　　If all men count with you, but none too much;
If you can fill the unforgiving minute
　　With sixty seconds' worth of distance run,
Yours is the Earth and everything that's in it,
　　And — which is more — you'll be a Man, my son!

My Boy Jack
1916
Rudyard Kipling

Rudyard Kipling's son, Jack, was lost in action during the Battle of Loos in September 1915. 'My son was killed while laughing at some jest,' he wrote some four years later. 'I would I knew what it was and it might serve me in a time when jests are few.' As an adviser to the Imperial War Graves Commission, Kipling chose the phrase 'A Soldier of the Great War, known unto God', to be inscribed on the headstones of unknown soldiers.

'Have you news of my boy Jack?'
Not this tide.
'When d'you think that he'll come back?'
Not with this wind blowing, and this tide.

'Has any one else had word of him?'
Not this tide.
For what is sunk will hardly swim,
Not with this wind blowing, and this tide.

'Oh, dear, what comfort can I find?'
None this tide,
Nor any tide,
Except he did not shame his kind —
Not even with that wind blowing, and that tide.

Then hold your head up all the more,
This tide,
And every tide;
Because he was the son you bore,
And gave to that wind blowing and that tide!

'Loveliest of trees, the cherry now'
from A Shropshire Lad
——— 1896 ———

A. E. HOUSMAN

IN HIS BOOK about A. E. Housman, the *Scholar Poet*, Richard Graves describes him as 'that sad, compassionate, loving, romantic man'.

> Loveliest of trees, the cherry now
> Is hung with bloom along the bough,
> And stands about the woodland ride
> Wearing white for Eastertide.
>
> Now, of my threescore years and ten,
> Twenty will not come again,
> And take from seventy springs a score,
> It only leaves me fifty more.
>
> And since to look at things in bloom
> Fifty springs are little room,
> About the woodlands I will go
> To see the cherry hung with snow.

Fern Hill
1946
DYLAN THOMAS

D YLAN THOMAS WAS 32 when he wrote this poem about his uncle and aunt's farm in Carmarthenshire. It conjures the magic of childhood with incredible energy and delight.

Now as I was young and easy under the apple boughs
About the lilting house and happy as the grass was green,
   The night above the dingle starry,
      Time let me hail and climb
   Golden in the heydays of his eyes,
And honoured among the wagons I was prince of the apple towns
And once below a time I lordly had the trees and leaves
      Trail with daisies and barley
   Down the rivers of the windfall light.

And as I was green and carefree, famous among the barns
About the happy yard and singing as the farm was home,
   In the sun that is young once only,
      Time let me play and be
   Golden in the mercy of his means,
And green and golden I was huntsman and herdsman, the calves
Sang to my horn, the foxes on the hills barked clear and cold,
      And the sabbath rang slowly
   In the pebbles of the holy streams.

All the sun long it was running, it was lovely, the hay
Fields high as the house, the tunes from the chimneys, it was air
   And playing, lovely and watery
      And fire green as grass.
   And nightly under the simple stars
As I rode to sleep the owls were bearing the farm away,

All the moon long I heard, blessed among stables, the nightjars
  Flying with the ricks, and the horses
    Flashing into the dark.

And then to awake, and the farm, like a wanderer white
With the dew, come back, the cock on his shoulder: it was all
  Shining, it was Adam and maiden,
    The sky gathered again
  And the sun grew round that very day.
So it must have been after the birth of the simple light
In the first, spinning place, the spellbound horses walking warm
  Out of the whinnying green stable
    On to the fields of praise.

And honoured among foxes and pheasants by the gay house
Under the new made clouds and happy as the heart was long,
  In the sun born over and over,
    I ran my heedless ways,
  My wishes raced through the house high hay
And nothing I cared, at my sky blue trades, that time allows
In all his tuneful turning so few and such morning songs
  Before the children green and golden
    Follow him out of grace.

Nothing I cared, in the lamb white days, that time would take me
Up to the swallow thronged loft by the shadow of my hand,
  In the moon that is always rising,
    Nor that riding to sleep
  I should hear him fly with the high fields
And wake to the farm forever fled from the childless land.
Oh as I was young and easy in the mercy of his means,
    Time held me green and dying
  Though I sang in my chains like the sea.

Home Thoughts from Abroad
1845

ROBERT BROWNING

BORN IN LONDON in 1812, Browning was educated in his father's library at home. He did try London University in 1828 but left in his second term. He spent much of his life abroad, which must have honed his appreciation of England, and though he is buried in Westminster Abbey, he died in Venice in 1889.

Oh, to be in England
Now that April's there,
And whoever wakes in England
Sees, some morning, unaware,
That the lowest boughs and the brushwood sheaf
Round the elm-tree bole are in tiny leaf,
While the chaffinch sings on the orchard bough
In England — now!

And after April, when May follows,
And the whitethroat builds, and all the swallows!
Hark, where my blossomed pear-tree in the hedge
Leans to the field and scatters on the clover
Blossoms and dewdrops — at the bent spray's edge —
That's the wise thrush; he sings each song twice over,
Lest you should think he never could recapture
The first fine careless rapture!
And though the fields look rough with hoary dew
All will be gay when noontide wakes anew
The buttercups, the little children's dower
 — Far brighter than this gaudy melon-flower!

The Old Vicarage, Grantchester
⟹ 1912 ⟸
RUPERT BROOKE

RUPERT BROOKE WROTE this poem in Berlin, when he was 25. He had settled in Grantchester, a few miles down the Cam from Cambridge University, in 1909, the year in which he began to publish his poetry.

> Just now the lilac is in bloom,
> All before my little room;
> And in my flower-beds, I think,
> Smile the carnation and the pink;
> And down the borders, well I know,
> The poppy and the pansy blow . . .
> Oh! there the chestnuts, summer through,
> Beside the river make for you
> A tunnel of green gloom, and sleep
> Deeply above; and green and deep
> The stream mysterious glides beneath,
> Green as a dream and deep as death.
> — Oh, damn! I know it! and I know
> How the May fields all golden show,
> And when the day is young and sweet,
> Gild gloriously the bare feet
> That run to bathe . . .
>
> [.....]
>
> Ah God! to see the branches stir
> Across the moon at Grantchester!
> To smell the thrilling-sweet and rotten
> Unforgettable, unforgotten
> River-smell, and hear the breeze

Sobbing in the little trees.
Say, do the elm-clumps greatly stand
Still guardians of that holy land?
The chestnuts shade, in reverend dream,
The yet unacademic stream?
Is dawn a secret shy and cold
Anadyomene, silver-gold?
And sunset still a golden sea
From Haslingfield to Madingley?
And after, ere the night is born,
Do hares come out about the corn?
Oh, is the water sweet and cool,
Gentle and brown, above the pool?
And laughs the immortal river still
Under the mill, under the mill?
Say, is there Beauty yet to find?
And Certainty? and Quiet kind?
Deep meadows yet, for to forget
The lies, and truths, and pain? . . . oh! yet
Stands the Church clock at ten to three?
And is there honey still for tea?

The Soldier

⸺ 1914 ⸺

Rupert Brooke

Brooke's five War Sonnets, including 'The Soldier', were first published in *New Numbers* in 1915, and he was instantly hailed as a new 'poet of war' – or 'war poet'.

If I should die, think only this of me:
    That there's some corner of a foreign field
That is for ever England. There shall be
    In that rich earth a richer dust concealed;
A dust whom England bore, shaped, made aware,
    Gave, once, her flowers to love, her ways to roam,
A body of England's, breathing English air,
    Washed by the rivers, blest by suns of home.
And think, this heart, all evil shed away,
    A pulse in the eternal mind, no less
        Gives somewhere back the thoughts by England given;
Her sights and sounds; dreams happy as her day;
    And laughter, learnt of friends; and gentleness,
        In hearts at peace, under an English heaven.

From Elegy Written in a Country Churchyard
⟹ 1751 ⟸
THOMAS GRAY

THOMAS GRAY WAS born in 1716 and educated at Eton and then Cambridge, where he remained for the rest of his life. Fascinated by Old Norse and Welsh poetry, and nature, he originally wrote poetry in Latin, then started to produce verse in English in the 1740s. He was offered the Poet Laureateship in 1757, but declined. He died in 1771.

On the eve of the attack on Quebec in 1759 General Wolfe recited this poem in its entirety – in order 'to soothe the men', telling them that he would 'prefer being the author of that poem to the glory of beating the French tomorrow'.

> The curfew tolls the knell of parting day,
> The lowing herd wind slowly o'er the lea,
> The ploughman homeward plods his weary way,
> And leaves the world to darkness and to me.
>
> Now fades the glimmering landscape on the sight,
> And all the air a solemn stillness holds,
> Save where the beetle wheels his droning flight,
> And drowsy tinklings lull the distant folds:
>
> Save that from yonder ivy-mantled tower
> The moping owl does to the moon complain
> Of such as, wandering near her secret bower,
> Molest her ancient solitary reign.
>
> Beneath those rugged elms, that yew-tree's shade,
> Where heaves the turf in many a mouldering heap,
> Each in his narrow cell for ever laid,
> The rude forefathers of the hamlet sleep.

The breezy call of incense-breathing morn,
The swallow twittering from the straw-built shed,
The cock's shrill clarion or the echoing horn,
No more shall rouse them from their lowly bed.

For them no more the blazing hearth shall burn,
Or busy housewife ply her evening care:
No children run to lisp their sire's return,
Or climb his knees the envied kiss to share.

Oft did the harvest to their sickle yield,
Their furrow oft the stubborn glebe has broke;
How jocund did they drive their team afield!
How bow'd the woods beneath their sturdy stroke!

Let not Ambition mock their useful toil,
Their homely joys, and destiny obscure;
Nor Grandeur hear, with a disdainful smile,
The short and simple annals of the poor.

Recently Become Cool
2004
GEORGE COURTAULD

M Y OLDEST SON wrote this at school about his mother. It is my favourite poem.

She has
Kind blue eyes
Hair blond,
Long
Freckles dotted over,
Determined chin,
Small nose,
Rosy cheeks,
Make the rest of the face.

Watches our matches,
Pink overcoat,
Boots.
Shame gurgles down my throat,
But still I say 'that's my mum'.

Recently become cool,
Baker boy hat,
Large black boots,
Usually says
'I've had this for ages!'
We know it's new!

Time!
No worry to her!
Late. 'Who cares?'
She usually says.
She's not shy.
Says what she thinks,
But
Usually gets on with things.

Thinks her phone's her best friend.
She's on it the whole time,
'Shut up! Be quiet!'
There's no getting her off.

Likes a laugh
Loves to jig to the Bee Gees.
Still works
Very hard.
She still finds time to help us,
Others,
On top of work,
College,
Clinic.

Keeps a straight face when
Times are hard.
Underneath stress peeps
Through.

Tennis! Don't mention it.
Plays a lot, rather good, goes to
The Gym.
Always dieting,
Atkins,
Weight Watchers,
Slim Fast,
Whatever,
She's done it.

Always supportive,
Always there,
Loves us, always will,
Know we're lucky.

ACKNOWLEDGEMENTS

The author and publishers would like to thank the following for permission to reproduce the following copyright material.

The Barbara Levy Literary Agency for 'Everyone Sang' by Siegfried Sassoon from *Collected Poems* (p10).

Faber & Faber Ltd for 'Lovesong' from *Crow* and 'The Thought Fox' from *Collected Poems* by Ted Hughes (p40, p116); 'Funeral Blues' from *Twelve Songs* and 'Sonnet VIII' (In Time of War) from *The English Auden* by W. H. Auden (p173, p30); 'Going, Going' and 'The Trees' from *High Windows* and 'Breadfruit' from *Collected Poems* by Philip Larkin (p21, p174, p33).

John Murray Publishers Ltd for 'A Subaltern's Love Song' and 'Christmas' from *Collected Poems* by John Betjeman (p47, p65).

The Literary Trustees of Walter de la Mare and the Society of Authors for 'The Listeners' and 'All That's Past' from *The Complete Poems of Walter de la Mare* by Walter de la Mare (p108, p110).

Marvell Press for 'Church Going' from *The Less Deceived* and 'In times where nothing stood' by Philip Larkin (p79, p158).

PFD on behalf of the Estate of Hilaire Belloc for 'Lines to a Don' from *Complete Verse* (p68).

Winston S. Chuchill and The Lady Soames for 'Poor Puggy-wug' from *A Thread in the Tapestry* (p78).

INDEX OF FIRST LINES